SG24-4986-00

IBM   International Technical Support Organization

Understanding LDAP

June 1998

> **Take Note!**
>
> Before using this information and the product it supports, be sure to read the general information in Appendix D, "Special Notices" on page 161.

First Edition (June 1998)

Comments may be addressed to:
IBM Corporation, International Technical Support Organization
Dept. JN9B Building 045 Internal Zip 2834
11400 Burnet Road
Austin, Texas 78758-3493

When you send information to IBM, you grant IBM a non-exclusive right to use or distribute the information in any way it believes appropriate without incurring any obligation to you.

Contents

Figures

Tables

Preface

Lightweight Directory Access Protocol (LDAP) is a fast growing technology for accessing common directory information. LDAP has been embraced and implemented in most network-oriented middleware. As an open, vendor-neutral standard, LDAP provides an extendable architecture for centralized storage and management of information that needs to be available for today's distributed systems and services.

After a fast start, it can be assumed that LDAP has become the de facto access method for directory information, much the same as the Domain Name System (DNS) is used for IP address look-up on almost any system on an intranet and on the Internet. LDAP is currently supported in most network operating systems, groupware and even shrink-wrapped network applications.

This book was written for those readers who need to understand the basic principles and concepts of LDAP. Some background knowledge about heterogeneous, distributed systems is assumed and highly beneficial when reading this book. This book is not meant to be an LDAP implementation guide, nor does it contain product-related or vendor-specific information other than as used in examples.

The Team That Wrote This Redbook

This redbook was produced by a team of specialists from around the world working at the International Technical Support Organization, Austin Center.

Heinz Johner is an Advisory Systems Engineer at the International Technical Support Organization, Austin Center. He writes extensively on all areas of the Distributed Computing Environment (DCE). Before joining the ITSO, he worked in the services organization of IBM Switzerland and was responsible for DCE and Systems Management in medium and large customer projects.

Larry Brown, Ph.D. is a Professional Services Technical Consultant for Transarc Corporation in the United States. He has 15 years of experience in the software industry and received his degree in Computer Engineering from Florida Atlantic University. His areas of expertise include distributed systems and transaction processing.

Franz-Stefan Hinner is a Systems Engineer at the Technical Marketing & Sales Support in Germany. He has been with IBM for 12 years. His areas of expertise include Network Operating Systems, like Warp Server, Windows NT

Novell NetWare, Distributed Computing Environment (DCE), Directory & Security Services (DSS), and Global Sign-On (GSO).

Wolfgang Reis is a Software Specialist from the AIX Customer Support Center in Germany. He has two years of experience supporting the IBM Internet products. He holds a degree in Physics received from the University of Bonn in Germany. His areas of expertise include the products Lotus Notes and Domino.

Johan Westman is an RS/6000 Technical Specialist working for IBM in Sweden. He has worked three years with RS/6000s, focusing on Network Computing. He holds a Master of Science in Engineering Physics degree from Uppsala University in Sweden. His main area of expertise is Network Computing solutions on IBM Midrange Server platforms.

Thanks to the following people for their invaluable contributions to this project:

Ellen Stokes
Lead Directory Architect, IETF participant, IBM Austin

Mike Schlosser
Senior Software Engineer, LDAP Design & Architecture, IETF participant, IBM Austin

Members of the LDAP planning and development team at IBM Austin:
Jamil Bissar
Mike Dugan
Mike Garrison
James Manon
Mark McConaughy

Special thanks go to the editors for their help in finalizing the text and publishing the book:

Marcus Brewer
Tara Campbell
John Weiss

Comments Welcome

Your comments are important to us!

We want our redbooks to be as helpful as possible. Please send us your comments about this or other redbooks in one of the following ways:

- Fax the evaluation form found in "ITSO Redbook Evaluation" on page 177 to the fax number shown on the form.

- Use the electronic evaluation form found on the Redbooks Web sites:

  | For Internet users | http://www.redbooks.ibm.com |
  | For IBM Intranet users | http://w3.itso.ibm.com |

- Send us a note at the following address:

  redbook@us.ibm.com

Chapter 1. LDAP: The New Common Directory

People and businesses are increasingly relying on networked computer systems to support distributed applications. These distributed applications might interact with computers on the same local area network (LAN), within a corporate intranet, or anywhere on the worldwide Internet. To improve functionality, ease of use and to enable cost-effective administration of distributed applications information about the services, resources, users, and other objects accessible from the applications needs to be organized in a clear and consistent manner. Much of this information can be shared among many applications, but it must also be protected to prevent unauthorized modification or the disclosure of private information.

Information describing the various users, applications, files, printers, and other resources accessible from a network is often collected into a special database, sometimes called a directory. As the number of different networks and applications has grown, the number of specialized directories of information has also grown, resulting in islands of information that cannot be shared and are difficult to maintain. If all of this information could be maintained and accessed in a consistent and controlled manner, it would provide a focal point for integrating a distributed environment into a consistent and seamless system.

The Lightweight Directory Access Protocol (LDAP) is an open industry standard that has evolved to meet these needs. LDAP defines a standard method for accessing and updating information in a directory. LDAP is gaining wide acceptance as the directory access method of the Internet and is therefore also becoming strategic within corporate intranets. It is being supported by a growing number of software vendors and is being incorporated into a growing number of applications.

Understanding LDAP explains the ideas behind LDAP and is intended to give the reader a detailed understanding of the architecture, use, and benefits of LDAP. Product-specific programming, configuration, and administration information is not presented; instead, the underlying concepts are discussed.

Chapter 1 provides background information about what a directory service is and the benefits it can provide. The architecture of LDAP is discussed in detail in Chapter 2. Chapter 3 discusses issues related to the design and maintenance of an LDAP directory. Building directory-enabled applications is discussed in Chapter 4, which presents the LDAP programming model and code examples. Finally, the future of LDAP is discussed in Chapter 5. Various reference material is collected in the appendices.

1.1 What is a Directory?

A directory is a listing of information about objects arranged in some order that gives details about each object. Common examples are a city telephone directory and a library card catalog. For a telephone directory, the objects listed are people; the names are arranged alphabetically, and the details given about each person are address and telephone number. Books in a library card catalog are ordered by author or by title, and information such as the ISBN number of the book and other publication information is given.

In computer terms, a directory is a specialized database, also called a data repository, that stores typed and ordered information about objects. A particular directory might list information about printers (the objects) consisting of typed information such as location (a formatted character string), speed in pages per minute (numeric), print streams supported (for example PostScript or ASCII), and so on.

Directories allow users or applications to find resources that have the characteristics needed for a particular task. For example, a directory of users can be used to look up a person's e-mail address or fax number. A directory could be searched to find a nearby PostScript color printer. Or a directory of application servers could be searched to find a server that can access customer billing information.

The terms *white pages* and *yellow pages* are sometimes used to describe how a directory is used. If the name of an object (person, printer) is known, its characteristics (phone number, pages per minute) can be retrieved. This is similar to looking up a name in the white pages of a telephone directory. If the name of a particular individual object is not known, the directory can be searched for a list of objects that meet a certain requirement. This is like looking up a listing of hairdressers in the yellow pages of a telephone directory. However, directories stored on a computer are much more flexible than the yellow pages of a telephone directory because they can usually be searched by specific criteria, not just by a predefined set of categories.

1.1.1 Differences Between Directories and Databases

A directory is often described as a database, but it is a specialized database that has characteristics that set it apart from general purpose relational databases. One special characteristic of directories is that they are accessed (read or searched) much more often than they are updated (written). Hundreds of people might look up an individual's phone number, or thousands of print clients might look up the characteristics of a particular printer. But the phone number or printer characteristics rarely change.

Because directories must be able to support high volumes of read requests, they are typically optimized for read access. Write access might be limited to system administrators or to the owner of each piece of information. A general purpose database, on the other, hand needs to support applications such as airline reservation and banking with high update volumes.

Because directories are meant to store relatively static information and are optimized for that purpose, they are not appropriate for storing information that changes rapidly. For example, the number of jobs currently in a print queue probably should not be stored in the directory entry for a printer because that information would have to be updated frequently to be accurate. Instead, the directory entry for the printer could contain the network address of a print server. The print server could be queried to learn the current queue length if desired. The information in the directory (the print server address) is static, whereas the number of jobs in the print queue is dynamic.

Another important difference between directories and general purpose databases is that directories may not support transactions (some vendor implementations, however, do). Transactions are all-or-nothing operations that must be completed in total or not at all. For example, when transferring money from one bank account to another, the money must be debited from one account and credited to the other account in a single transaction. If only half of this transaction completes or someone accesses the accounts while the money is in transit, the accounts will not balance. General-purpose databases usually support such transactions, which complicates their implementation.

Because directories deal mostly with read requests, the complexities of transactions can be avoided. If two people exchange offices, both of their directory entries need to be updated with new phone numbers, office locations, and so on. If one directory entry is updated, and then other directory entry is updated there is a brief period during which the directory will show that both people have the same phone number. Because updates are relatively rare, such anomalies are considered acceptable.

The type of information stored in a directory usually does not require strict consistency. It might be acceptable if information such as a telephone number is temporarily out of date. Because directories are not transactional, it is not a good idea to use them to store information sensitive to inconsistencies, like bank account balances.

Because general-purpose databases must support arbitrary applications such as banking and inventory control, they allow arbitrary collections of data to be stored. Directories may be limited in the type of data they allow to be stored (although the architecture does not impose such a limitation). For example, a directory specialized for customer contact information might be limited to storing only personal information such as names, addresses, and phone numbers. If a directory is extensible, it can be configured to store a variety of types of information, making it more useful to a variety of programs.

Another important difference between a directory and a general-purpose database is in the way information can be accessed. Most databases support a standardized, very powerful access method called Structured Query Language (SQL). SQL allows complex update and query functions at the cost of program size and application complexity. LDAP directories, on the other hand, use a simplified and optimized access protocol that can be used in slim and relatively simple applications.

Because directories are not intended to provide as many functions as general-purpose databases, they can be optimized to economically provide more applications with rapid access to directory data in large distributed environments. Because the intended use of directories is restricted to a read-mostly, nontransactional environment, both the directory client and directory server can be simplified and optimized.

What About the Future?

Many of the differences just mentioned may lead to the suspicion that a directory is no more than a limited-function database. This is in deed partly true, since one of the important design goals of a directory service is that it can be accessed and used from relatively small and simple applications. In fact, certain vendor products, such as IBM's eNetwork LDAP Directory, use a relational database under the cover to implement the functions. Also, proposals are being discussed in the standards bodies to add some functions to future versions of LDAP that currently are specific to databases, such as support for transactional updates.

1.1.2 Directory Clients and Servers

Directories are usually accessed using the client/server model of communication. An application that wants to read or write information in a directory does not access the directory directly. Instead, it calls a function or application programming interface (API) that causes a message to be sent to another process. This second process accesses the information in the directory on behalf of the requesting application. The results of the read or write are then returned to the requesting application (see Figure 1).

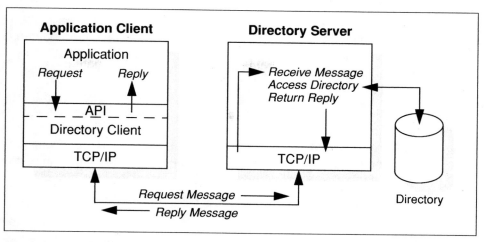

Figure 1. Directory Client/Server Interaction

The request is performed by the directory client, and the process that looks up information in the directory is called the directory server. In general, servers provide a specific service to clients. Sometimes a server might become the client of other servers in order to gather the information necessary to process a request.

A directory service is only one type of service that might be available in a client/server environment. Other common examples of services are file services, mail services, print services, Web page services, and so on. The client and server processes might or might not be on the same machine. A server is capable of serving many clients. Some servers can process client requests in parallel. Other servers queue incoming client requests for serial processing if they are currently busy processing another client's request.

An API defines the programming interface a particular programming language uses to access a service. The format and contents of the messages exchanged between client and server must adhere to an agreed upon protocol. LDAP defines a message protocol used by directory clients and directory servers. There is also an associated LDAP API for the C language and ways to access LDAP from withing a Java application (see Chapter 4, "Building LDAP-Enabled Applications" on page 85, for more details on these APIs). The client is not dependent upon a particular implementation of the server, and the server can implement the directory however it chooses.

1.1.3 Distributed Directories

The terms local, global, centralized, and distributed are often used to describe a directory or directory service. These terms mean different things to different people in different contexts. In this section, these terms are explained as they apply to directories in different contexts.

In general, local means something is close by, and global means that something is spread across the universe of interest. The universe of interest might be a company, a country, or the Earth. Local and global are two ends of a continuum. That is, something may be more or less global or local than something else. Centralized means that something is in one place, and distributed means that something is in more than one place. Like local and global, something can be distributed to a greater or lesser extent.

The information stored in a directory can be local or global in scope. For example, a directory that stores local information might consist of the names, e-mail addresses, public encryption keys, and so on of members of a department or workgroup. A directory that stores global information might store information for an entire company. Here, the universe of interest is the company.

The clients that access information in the directory can be local or global. Local clients might all be located in the same building or on the same LAN. Global clients might be distributed across the continent or planet.

The directory itself can be centralized or distributed. If a directory is centralized, there is one directory server that provides access to the directory. If the directory is distributed, there is more that one server that provides access to the directory. When people refer to a distributed directory, they are usually referring to distributed directory servers.

When a directory is distributed, the information stored in the directory can be partitioned or replicated. When information is partitioned, each directory server stores a unique and non-overlapping subset of the information. That is, each directory entry is stored by one and only one server. When information is replicated, the same directory entry is stored by more than one server. In a distributed directory, some information may be partitioned, and some information may be replicated.

The three "dimensions" of a directory — scope of information, location of clients, and distribution of servers — are independent of each other. For example, clients scattered across the globe could access a directory containing only information about a single department, and that directory could be replicated at many directory servers. Or clients in a single location could access a directory containing information about everybody in the world that is stored by a single directory server.

The scope of information to be stored in a directory is often given as an application requirement. The distribution of directory servers and the way in which data is partitioned or replicated can often be controlled to effect the performance and availability of the directory. For example, a distributed and replicated directory might perform better because a read request can be serviced by a nearby server. A centralized directory may be less available because it is a single point of failure. However, a distributed directory might be more difficult to maintain because multiple sites, possibly under the control of multiple administrators, must be kept up-to-date and in running order.

The design and maintenance of a directory service can be complex, and many trade-offs are involved. This topic is discussed in more detail in Chapter 3, "Designing and Maintaining an LDAP Directory" on page 57.

1.1.4 Directory Security

The security of information stored in a directory is a major consideration. Some directories are meant to be accessed publicly on the Internet, but any user should not necessarily be able to perform any operation. A company's directory servicing its intranet can be stored behind a firewall to keep the general public from accessing it, but more security control is needed within the intranet itself.

For example, anybody should be able to look up an employee's e-mail address, but only the employee or a system administrator should be able to change it. Members of the personnel department might have permission to look up an employee's home telephone number, but their co-workers might not. Perhaps information needs to be encrypted before being transmitted over the network. A security policy defines who has what type of access to what information. The security policy is defined by the organization that maintains the directory.

A directory should support the basic capabilities needed to implement a security policy. The directory might not directly provide the underlying security capabilities, but it might be integrated with a trusted network security service that provides the basic security services. First, a method is needed to authenticate users. Authentication verifies that users are who they say they are. A user name and password is a basic authentication scheme. Once users are authenticated, it must be determined if they have the authorization or permission to perform the requested operation on the specific object.

Authorization is often based on access control lists (ACLs). An ACL is a list of authorizations that may be attached to objects and attributes in the directory. An ACL lists what type of access each user is allowed. In order to make ACLs shorter and more manageable, users with the same access rights are often put into security groups. Table 1 shows an example ACL for an employee's directory entry.

Table 1. Example ACL for an Employee's Directory Entry

User or Group	Access Rights
owner	read, modify (but not delete)
administrators	all
personnel	read all fields
all others	read restricted

Security is discussed in more detail in 2.3, "Security" on page 43.

1.2 The Directory as Infrastructure

A directory that is accessible by all applications is a vital part of the infrastructure supporting a distributed system. A directory service provides a single logical view of the users, resources, and other objects that make up a distributed system. This allows users and applications to access network resources transparently. That is, the system is perceived as an integrated whole, not a collection of independent parts. Objects can be accessed by name or function without knowing low-level identifiers such as host addresses, file server names, and e-mail addresses.

1.2.1 Directory-Enabled Applications

A directory-enabled application is an application that uses a directory service to improve its functionality, ease of use, and administration. Today many applications make use of information that could be stored in a directory. For example, consider a group calendar application that is used to schedule meetings of company personnel in different conference rooms.

In the worst case, the calendar application does not use a directory service at all. If this were the case, a user trying to schedule a meeting would have to remember the room number of every conference room that might be appropriate for the meeting. Is the room big enough, does it have the necessary audio and video equipment, and so on? The user would also have to remember the names and e-mail addresses of every attendee that needs to receive a meeting notice. Such an application would obviously be difficult to use.

If conference room information (size, location, special equipment, and so on) and personnel information (name, e-mail address, phone number, and so on) could be accessed from a directory service, the application would be much easier to use. Also, the functionality of the application could be improved. For example, a list of all available conference rooms meeting the size and equipment requirements could be presented to the user.

But the developers of directory-enabled applications are faced with a problem. What if they cannot assume that a directory service will exist in all environments? If there is a directory service it might be specific to a certain network operating system (NOS), making the application non-portable. Can the existing directory service be extended to store the type of information needed by the application? Because of these concerns, application developers often took the approach of developing their own application-specific directory.

1.2.2 The Benefits of a Common Directory

An application-specific directory stores only the information needed by a particular application and is not accessible by other applications. Because a full-function directory service is complex to build, application-specific directories are typically very limited. They probably store only a specific type of information, probably do not have general search capabilities, probably do not support replication and partitioning, and probably do not have a full set of administration tools. An application-specific directory could be as simple as a set of editable text files, or it could be stored and accessed in an undocumented, proprietary manner.

In such an environment, each application creates and manages its own application-specific directory. This quickly becomes an administrative nightmare. The same e-mail address stored by the calendar application might also be stored by a mail application and by an application that notifies system operators of equipment problems. Keeping multiple copies of information up-to-date and synchronized is difficult, especially when different user interfaces and even different system administrators are involved.

What is needed is a common, application-independent directory. If application developers could be assured of the existence of a directory service, then application-specific directories would not be necessary. However, a common directory must address the problems mentioned above. It must be based on an open standard that is supported by many vendors on many platforms. It must be accessible through a standard API. It must be extensible so that it can hold the types of data needed by arbitrary applications. And it must provide full functionality without requiring excessive resources on smaller systems. Since more users and applications will access and depend on the common directory, it must also be robust, secure and scalable.

When such a directory infrastructure is in place, application developers can devote their time to developing applications instead of application-specific directories. In the same way that developers rely on the communications infrastructure of TCP/IP, remote procedure call (RPC), and object request brokers (ORBs) to free them from low-level communication issues, they will be able to rely on powerful, full-function directory services. LDAP is the protocol to be used to access this common directory infrastructure. Like HTTP (hypertext transfer protocol) and FTP (file transfer protocol), LDAP will become an indispensable part of the Internet's protocol suite.

When applications access a standard common directory that is designed in a proper way, rather than using application-specific directories, redundant and costly administration can be eliminated, and security risks are more controllable. The calendar, mail, and operator notification applications can all access the same directory to retrieve an email address. New uses for directory information will be realized, and a synergy will develop as more applications take advantage of the common directory.

1.3 LDAP History and Standards

In the 1970s, the integration of communications and computing technologies led to the development of new communication technologies. Many of the proprietary systems that were developed were incompatible with other systems. It became apparent that standards were needed to allow equipment and systems from different vendors to interoperate. Two independent major standardizations efforts developed to define such standards.

1.3.1 OSI and the Internet

One standards drive was lead by the CCITT (Comite Consultatif International Telephonique et Telegraphique, or Consultative Committee on International Telephony and Telegraphy), and the ISO (International Standards Organization). The CCITT has since become the ITU-T (International Telecommunications Union - Telecommunication Standardization Sector). This effort resulted in the OSI (Open Systems Interconnect) Reference Model (ISO 7498), which defined a seven-layer model of data communication with physical transport at the lower layer and application protocols at the upper layers.

The other standards drive grew up around the Internet and developed from research sponsored by DARPA (the Defense Advanced Research Projects Agency) in the United States. The Internet Architecture Board (IAB) and its subsidiary, the Internet Engineering Task Force (IETF), develop standards for the Internet in the form of documents called RFC's (Request for Comments), which after being approved, implemented, and used for a period of time, eventually become standards (STDs). Before a proposal becomes an RFC, it is called an Internet Draft.

The two standards processes approach standardization from two different perspectives. The OSI approach started from a clean slate and defined standards using a formal committee process without requiring implementations. The Internet uses a less formal engineering approach, where anybody can propose and comment on RFCs, and implementations are required to verify feasibility.

The OSI protocols developed slowly, and because running the full protocol stack, is resource intensive, they have not been widely deployed, especially in the desktop and small computer market. In the meantime, TCP/IP and the Internet were developing rapidly and being put into use. Also, some network vendors developed proprietary network protocols and products.

1.3.2 X.500: The Directory Service Standard

However, the OSI protocols did address issues important in large distributed systems that were developing in an ad hoc manner in the desktop and Internet marketplace. One such important area was directory services. The CCITT created the X.500 standard in 1988, which became *ISO 9594, Data Communications Network Directory, Recommendations X.500-X.521* in 1990, though it is still commonly referred to as X.500.

X.500 organizes directory entries in a hierarchal name space capable of supporting large amounts of information. It also defines powerful search capabilities to make retrieving information easier. Because of its functionality and scalability, X.500 is often used together with add-on modules for interoperation between incompatible directory services.

X.500 specifies that communication between the directory client and the directory server uses the directory access protocol (DAP). However, as an application layer protocol, the DAP requires the entire OSI protocol stack to operate. Supporting the OSI protocol stack requires more resources than are available in many small environments. Therefore, an interface to an X.500 directory server using a less resource-intensive or lightweight protocol was desired.

1.3.3 LDAP: Lightweight Access to X.500

LDAP was developed as a lightweight alternative to DAP. LDAP requires the lighter weight and more popular TCP/IP protocol stack rather than the OSI protocol stack. LDAP also simplifies some X.500 operations and omits some esoteric features.

Two precursors to LDAP appeared as RFCs issued by the IETF, *Directory Assistance Service* (RFC 1202) and *DIXIE Protocol Specification* (RFC 1249). These were both informational RFCs which were not proposed as standards. The directory assistance service (DAS) defined a method by which a directory client could communicate to a proxy on a OSI-capable host which issued X.500 requests on the client's behalf. DIXIE is similar to DAS, but provides a more direct translation of the DAP.

The first version of LDAP was defined in *X.500 Lightweight Access Protocol* (RFC 1487), which was replaced by *Lightweight Directory Access Protocol* (RFC 1777). LDAP further refines the ideas and protocols of DAS and DIXIE. It is more implementation neutral and reduces the complexity of clients to encourage the deployment of directory-enabled applications. Much of the work on DIXIE and LDAP was carried out at the University of Michigan, which provides reference implementations of LDAP and maintains LDAP-related Web pages and mailing lists (see A.2, "The University of Michigan (UMICH)" on page 140).

RFC 1777 defines the LDAP protocol itself. RFC 1777, along with

- *The String Representation of Standard Attribute Syntaxes* (RFC 1778)

- *A String Representation of Distinguished Names* (RFC 1779)

- *An LDAP URL Format* (RFC 1959)

- *A String Representation of LDAP Search Filters* (RFC 1960)

define LDAP Version 2. See Chapter 2, "LDAP Concepts and Architecture" on page 19, for information about these topics.

LDAP Version 2 has reached the status of draft standard in the IETF standardization process, one step from being a standard. Although changes could be made to a draft standard, substantial and widespread testing of the draft standard is desired. Many vendors have implemented products that support LDAP Version 2 (see Appendix B, "LDAP Products and Services" on page 143). Some vendors are also implementing products that also support all or parts of LDAP Version 3.

LDAP Version 3 is defined by *Lightweight Directory Access Protocol (v3)* (RFC 2251). Related RFCs that are new or updated for LDAP Version 3 are:

- *Lightweight Directory Access Protocol (v3): Attribute Syntax Definitions* (RFC 2252)
- *Lightweight Directory Access Protocol (v3): UTF-8 String Representation of Distinguished Names* (RFC 2253)
- *The String Representation of LDAP Search Filters* (RFC 2254)
- *The LDAP URL Format* (RFC 2255)
- *A Summary of the X.500(96) User Schema for use with LDAPv3 (RFC 2256)*

RFC 2251 is a proposed standard, one step below a draft standard. Minor revisions of a proposed standard are likely, but testing by several groups is desired. LDAP V3 extends LDAP V2 in the following areas:

Referrals
A server that does not store the requested data can refer the client to another server.

Security
Extensible authentication using Simple Authentication and Security Layer (SASL) mechainism.

Internationalization
UTF-8 support for international characters.

Extensibility
New object types and operations can be dynamically defined and schema published in a standard manner.

Again, see Chapter 2, "LDAP Concepts and Architecture" on page 19, for information about these topics. In this book, the term LDAP generally refers to LDAP Version 3. Differences between LDAP Version 2 and LDAP Version 3 are noted when necessary.

LDAP defines the communication protocol between the directory client and server, but does not define a programming interface for the client. *The LDAP Application Program Interface* (RFC 1823) defines a C language API to access a directory using LDAP Version 2. This is an informational RFC, which means it is not an official standard. However, it has become a de facto standard. A standardized protocol and the availability of a common API on different platforms are the major reasons for the wide acceptance of LDAP. At the time of writing this book, RFC 1823 is in the process of being updated to support LDAP Version 3, but a new RFC number has not yet been assigned to the existing draft. See Chapter 4, "Building LDAP-Enabled Applications" on page 85 for information on using the LDAP API.

1.4 LDAP: Protocol or Directory?

LDAP defines a communication protocol. That is, it defines the transport and format of messages used by a client to access data in an X.500-like directory. LDAP does not define the directory service itself. Yet people often talk about LDAP directories. Others say LDAP is only a protocol, that there is no such thing as an LDAP directory. What is an LDAP directory?

An application client program initiates an LDAP message by calling an LDAP API. But an X.500 directory server does not understand LDAP messages. In fact, the LDAP client and X.500 server even use different communication protocols (TCP/IP vs. OSI). The LDAP client actually communicates with a gateway process (also called a proxy or front end) that forwards requests to the X.500 directory server (see Figure 2). This gateway is known as an LDAP server. It services requests from the LDAP client. It does this by becoming a client of the X.500 server. The LDAP server must communicate using both TCP/IP and OSI.

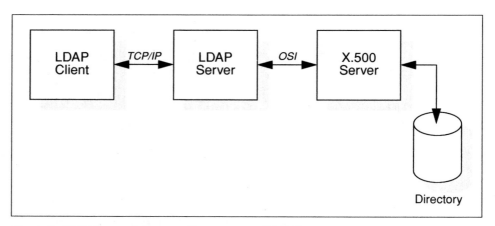

Figure 2. LDAP Server Acting as a Gateway to an X.500 Server

As the use of LDAP grew and its benefits became apparent, people who did not have X.500 servers or the environments to support them wanted to build directories that could be accessed by LDAP clients. So why not have the LDAP server store and access the directory itself instead of only acting as a gateway to X.500 servers (see Figure 3)? This eliminates any need for the OSI protocol stack. Of course this makes the LDAP server much more complicated since it must store and retrieve directory entries. These LDAP servers are often called stand-alone LDAP servers because they do not depend on an X.500 directory server. Since LDAP does not support all X.500 capabilities, a stand-alone LDAP server only needs to support the capabilities required by LDAP.

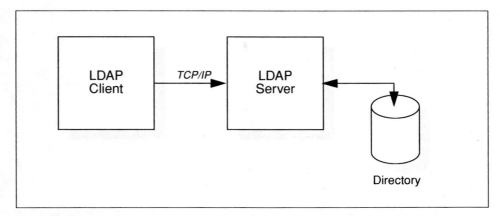

Figure 3. Stand-Alone LDAP Server

RFC 1777 (LDAP Version 2) discusses providing access to the X.500 directory. RFC 2251 (LDAP Version 3) discusses providing access to directories supporting the X.500 model. This change in language reflects the idea that an LDAP server can implement the directory itself or can be a gateway to an X.500 directory.

From the client's point of view, any server that implements the LDAP protocol is an LDAP directory server, whether the server actually implements the directory or is a gateway to an X.500 server. The directory that is accessed can be called an LDAP directory, whether the directory is implemented by a stand-alone LDAP server or by an X.500 server.

1.5 The LDAP Road Map

LDAP has evolved to meet the need of providing access to a common directory infrastructure. LDAP is an open industry standard that is supported by many system vendors on a variety of platforms. It is being incorporated into software products (see Appendix B, "LDAP Products and Services" on page 143) and is quickly becoming the directory access protocol of choice. LDAP allows products from different vendors on different platforms to interoperate and provide a global directory infrastructure, much like HTTP enabled the deployment of the World Wide Web.

Current LDAP products support at least LDAP Version 2. Many products already support parts or all of LDAP Version 3. Further enhancements beyond Version 3 are being discussed by the IETF (see Chapter 5, "The Future of LDAP" on page 131).

Application developers can take advantage of LDAP to develop next-generation directory-enabled applications. While X.500 has traditionally been deployed only in large organizations that can commit the resources necessary to support it, LDAP is also appropriate for small organizations. For example, a small company might want to exchange documents with its customers and suppliers using Electronic Data Interchange (EDI). EDI requires both parties to agree on the types of documents to be exchanged, communication requirements, and so on. Companies could publish their EDI characteristics in publicly accessible LDAP directories to facilitate EDI.

A common directory infrastructure encourages new uses. The Directory Enabled Networks (DEN) Initiative is a proposal to allow information about network configuration, protocol information, router characteristics, and so on to be stored in an LDAP directory. The availability of this information in a common format from many equipment vendors will allow the intelligent management and provisioning of network resources. These examples show the diverse uses of directory-enabled applications supported by a common directory infrastructure accessed with LDAP.

1.6 The Quick Start: A Public LDAP Example

Studying Internet Drafts, RFCs, and related publications about LDAP, including this book, may lead to the assumption that LDAP is still under construction, and it might be too early for a practical implementation. This is actually true, as far as proposed extensions and future enhancements are concerned; nevertheless, base sets for LDAP Version 2 and 3 are defined and ready to be used. Due to the nature of the process in which IETF standards emerge (as outlined in 1.3.1, "OSI and the Internet" on page 10), there will always be multiple parties working on different or even the same subjects.

LDAP is currently being used in many small- and large-scale implementations. If you have never encountered an actual LDAP implementation, take a look at the following example of a publicly accessible LDAP service.

Although LDAP directories can be used to store various kinds of information, the most obvious use is to implement a white pages directory of people to make their names, addresses, phone numbers, and so on available to anybody for searching and reading. In fact, there are several LDAP white pages available on the Internet. *Four11* (`www.four11.com`), a directory service provided by Yahoo!, for example, offers an LDAP access to its extensive people directory.

Modern Web browsers, such as Netscape's Communicator or Microsoft's Internet Explorer, on the other hand, are LDAP-enabled. This means that such a browser can look up entries in an LDAP directory. In the following example, we use Netscape Communicator to show how that fits together with public LDAP services. When you install Communicator, a series of public LDAP services are already configured as selectable directories for searching. Without any further configuration, you may use these directories right away by selecting **Search Directory** from the **Edit** pull-down in the Navigator window. Figure 4 shows the window that comes up. Notice the drop-down list for Internet directories, where the Four11 Directory is being selected for the subsequent search. Some other selections can be made in this window, such as whether you want to search for a name, an e-mail address or to add additional search criteria.

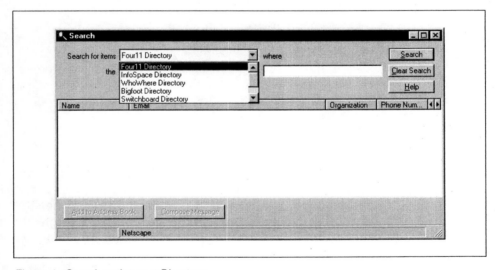

Figure 4. Search an Internet Directory

Once all fields are selected or filled as required, a click on the **Search** button sends the request to the selected service and returns the results in a short while.

Figure 5 shows the search results for people associated with the organization IBM and the city of Austin. Note that only the first 100 records are returned, which is a configurable option in your browser.

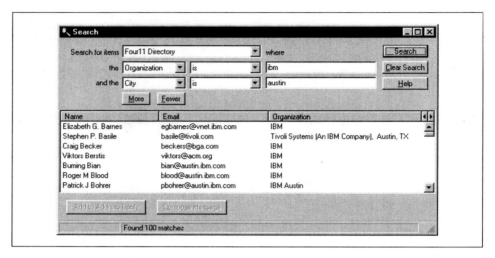

Figure 5. Results Searching an Internet Directory

What happens behind the scene is that the browser sends an LDAP search request to the selected service and retrieves the search results. As can be seen in this example, LDAP is already widely used and offered through the public Internet. Additional LDAP servers, for example in your organization, can be added to the browser's configuration.

No Connection to the LDAP Server?

If you try to reproduce the example above and get an error saying that the browser cannot connect to the LDAP server, then your system is most likely connected to a private intranet, and the firewall between this intranet and the Internet does not allow LDAP traffic to pass through. Try to run this example from a system that is directly connected to the Internet.

LDAP uses another connection port than, for example, the popular Hypertext Transfer Protocol (HTTP). While firewalls usually allow the passage of specific traffic, such as HTTP on port 80, there is a good chance that the LDAP port 389 is blocked by default in your installation.

Chapter 2. LDAP Concepts and Architecture

LDAP is based on the client/server model of distributed computing (see 1.1.2, "Directory Clients and Servers" on page 4). LDAP has evolved as a lightweight protocol for accessing information in X.500 directory services. It has since become more independent of X.500, and servers that specifically support the LDAP protocol rather than the X.500 Directory Access Protocol (DAP) are now common. The success of LDAP has been largely due to the following characteristics that make it simpler to implement and use, compared to X.500 and DAP:

- LDAP runs over TCP/IP rather than the OSI protocol stack. TCP/IP is less resource-intensive and is much more widely available, especially on desktop systems.

- The functional model of LDAP is simpler. It omits duplicate, rarely-used and esoteric features. This makes LDAP easier to understand and to implement.

- LDAP uses strings to represent data rather than complicated structured syntaxes such as ASN.1 (Abstract Syntax Notation One).

This chapter explains the basic architecture of LDAP. It discusses the information, naming, functional, and security models that form the basis of the LDAP architecture. Various terms and concepts defined by or needed to understand the LDAP architecture are introduced along the way. After a general overview of the architecture, each of the models that form the backbone of the LDAP architecture is discussed in detail.

2.1 Overview of LDAP Architecture

LDAP defines the content of messages exchanged between an LDAP client and an LDAP server. The messages specify the operations requested by the client (search, modify, delete, and so on), the responses from the server, and the format of data carried in the messages. LDAP messages are carried over TCP/IP, a connection-oriented protocol; so there are also operations to establish and disconnect a session between the client and server.

However, for the designer of an LDAP directory, it is not so much the structure of the messages being sent and received over the wire that is of interest. What is important is the logical model that is defined by these messages and data types, how the directory is organized, what operations are possible, how information is protected, and so forth.

The general interaction between an LDAP client and an LDAP server takes the following form:

- The client establishes a session with an LDAP server. This is known as *binding* to the server. The client specifies the host name or IP address and TCP/IP port number where the LDAP server is listening. The client can provide a user name and a password to properly authenticate with the server. Or the client can establish an anonymous session with default access rights. The client and server can also establish a session that uses stronger security methods such as encryption of data.

- The client then performs operations on directory data. LDAP offers both read and update capabilities. This allows directory information to be managed as well as queried. LDAP also supports searching the directory for data meeting arbitrary user-specified criteria. Searching is a very common operation in LDAP. A user can specify what part of the directory to search and what information to return. A search filter that uses Boolean conditions specifies what directory data matches the search.

- When the client is finished making requests, it closes the session with the server. This is also known as *unbinding*.

Although it is not defined by the LDAP protocol and architecture itself, there is a well-known LDAP API (application program interface) that allows applications to easily interact with LDAP servers. The API can be considered an extension to the LDAP architecture. Although the C language LDAP API is only an informational RFC and the most recent update to it is an Internet Draft, it has achieved de facto standard status because it is supported by all major LDAP vendors. The philosophy of the LDAP API is to keep simple things simple. This means that adding directory support to existing applications can be done with low overhead. As we will see in Chapter 4, "Building LDAP-Enabled Applications" on page 85, this interface is reasonably easy to use and implement in applications.

Because LDAP was originally intended as a lightweight alternative to DAP for accessing X.500 directories, it follows an X.500 model (see 1.3.2, "X.500: The Directory Service Standard" on page 11). The directory stores and organizes data structures known as *entries*.

A directory entry usually describes an object such as a person, a printer, a server, and so on. Each entry has a name called a distinguished name (DN) that uniquely identifies it. The DN consists of a sequence of parts called relative distinguished names (RDNs), much like a file name consists of a path of directory names in many operating systems such as UNIX and Windows. The entries can be arranged into a hierarchical tree-like structure based on their distinguished names. This tree of directory entries is called the Directory Information Tree (DIT).

Each entry contains one or more attributes that describe the entry. Each attribute has a type and a value. For example, the directory entry for a person might have an attribute called `telephonNnumber`. The syntax of the `telephoneNumber` attribute would specify that a telephone number must be a string of numbers that can contain spaces and hyphens. The value of the attribute would be the person's telephone number, such as 512-555-1212.

A directory entry describes some object. An object class is a general description, sometimes called a template, of an object as opposed to the description of a particular object. For instance, the object class person has a `surname` attribute, whereas the object describing John Smith has a surname attribute with the value Smith. The object classes that a directory server can store and the attributes they contain are described by schema. Schema define what object classes are allowed where in the directory, what attributes they must contain, what attributes are optional, and the syntax of each attribute. For example, a schema could define a person object class. The person schema might require that a person have a `surname` attribute that is a character string, specify that a person entry can optionally have a `telephoneNumber` attribute that is a string of numbers with spaces and hyphens, and so on.

LDAP defines operations for accessing and modifying directory entries such as:

- Searching for entries meeting user-specified criteria
- Adding an entry
- Deleting an entry
- Modifying an entry
- Modifying the distinguished name or relative distinguished name of an entry (move)
- Comparing an entry

LDAP is documented in several IETF RFCs. As discussed in 1.3.3, "LDAP: Lightweight Access to X.500" on page 12, the current version of LDAP is Version 3. That section also lists the RFCs associated with each version of LDAP.

The LDAP Version 3 RFCs are again listed below along with a short description to provide an overview of the documents defining the LDAP architecture.

1. RFC 2251 *Lightweight Directory Access Protocol (v3)*

   Describes the LDAP protocol designed to provide lightweight access to directories supporting the X.500 model. The lightweight protocol is meant to be implementable in resource-constrained environments such as browsers and small desktop systems. This RFC is the core of the LDAP family of RFCs. It describes how entries are named with distinguished names, defines the format of messages exchanged between client and server, enumerates the operations that can be performed by the client, and specifies that data is represented using UTF-8 character encoding.

   The RFC specifies that the schema describing directory entries must themselves be readable so that a client can determine what type of objects a directory server stores. It defines how the client can be referred to another LDAP server if a server does not contain the requested information. It describes how individual operations can be extended using controls and how additional operations can be defined using extensions. It also discusses how clients can authenticate to servers and optionally use Simple Authentication and Security Layer (SASL) to allow additional authentication mechanisms.

2. RFC 2252 *Lightweight Directory Access Protocol (v3): Attribute Syntax Definitions*

   LDAP uses octet strings to represent the values of attributes for transmission in the LDAP protocol. This RFC defines how values such as integers, time stamps, mail addresses, and so on are represented. For example, the integer 123 is represented by the string "123". These definitions are called attribute syntaxes. This RFC describes how an attribute with a syntax such as "telephone number" is encoded. It also defines matching rules to determine if values meet search criteria. An example is `caseIgnoreString`, which is used to compare character strings when case is not important.

   These attribute types and syntaxes are used to build schema that describe objects classes. A schema lists what attributes a directory entry must or may have. Every directory entry has an `objectclass` attribute that lists the (one or more) schema that describe the entry. For example, a directory entry could be described by the object classes `residentialPerson` and `organizationalPerson`. If an `objectclass` attribute includes the value `extensibleObject`, it can contain any attribute.

3. RFC 2253 *Lightweight Directory Access Protocol (v3): UTF-8 String Representation of Distinguished Names*

   Distinguished names (DNs) are the unique identifiers, sometimes called primary keys, of directory entries. X.500 uses ASN.1 to encode distinguished names. LDAP encodes distinguished names as strings. This RFC defines how distinguished names are represented as strings. A string representation is easy to encode and decode and is also human readable. A DN is composed of a sequence of relative distinguished names (RDNs) separated by commas. The sequence of RDNs making up a DN names the ancestors of a directory entry up to the root of the DIT. Each RDN is composed of an attribute value from the directory entry. For example, the DN cn=John Smith, ou=Austin, o=IBM, c=US represents a directory entry for a person with the common name (cn) John Smith under the organizational unit (ou) Austin in the organization (o) IBM in the country (c) US.

4. RFC 2254 *The String Representation of LDAP Search Filters*

   LDAP search filters provide a powerful mechanism to search a directory for entries that match specific criteria. The LDAP protocol defines the network representation of a search filter. This document defines how to represent a search filter as a human-readable string. Such a representation can be used by applications or in program source code to specify search criteria. Attribute values are compared using relational operators such as equal, greater than, or "sounds like" for approximate or phonetic matching. Boolean operators can be used to build more complex search filters. For example, the search filter (| (sn=Smith) (cn=Jo*)) searches for entries that either have a surname attribute of Smith or that have a common name attribute that begins with Jo.

5. RFC 2255 *The LDAP URL Format*

   Uniform Resource Locators (URLs) are used to identify Web pages, files, and other resources on the Internet. An LDAP URL specifies an LDAP search to be performed at a particular LDAP server. An LDAP URL represents in a compact and standard way the information returned as the result of the search. Section 4.4, "LDAP URLs" on page 120, explains LDAP URLs in detail.

6. RFC 2256 *A Summary of the X.500(96) User Schema for use with LDAPv3*

   Many schema and attributes commonly accessed by directory clients are already defined by X.500. This RFC provides an overview of those attribute types and object classes that LDAP servers should recognize. For instance, attributes such as cn (common name), description, and postalAddress are defined. Object classes such as country, organizationalUnit, groupOfNames, and applicationEntity are also defined.

The RFCs listed above build up the core LDAP Version 3 specification. In addition to these RFCs, the IETF lists a number of so-called proposed extensions to LDAP Version 3 that vendors may implement as well. However, these proposed extensions only have the status of Internet Drafts and may therefore still change. The following list summarizes some of these proposed extensions:

- Mandatory-to-Implement Authentication

  An attempt to have at least one standard, secure authentication method available in all servers and clients (not only LDAP), rather than individual methods for each protocol above TCP/IP.

- Extensions for Dynamic Directory Services

  This is a protocol extension that allows clients to interact more reliably with servers while directory contents are being changed.

- Use of Language Codes in LDAP

  Describes the addition of natural language codes to attributes stored in an LDAP directory.

- LDAPv3 Extension for Transport Layer Security

  Defines the integration of the Transport Layer Security (TLS) mechanism into LDAP.

- LDAP Control Extension for Simple Paged Results Manipulation

  Describes a control extension for paging of search results. This is of special value for simple, limited-function clients so they can request that search results are returned in smaller portions (pages) at a time.

- Referrals and Knowledge References in LDAP Directories

  Defines how referrals and reference information can be stored as attributes and how they may be used.

- LDAP Control Extension for Server Side Sorting of Search Results

  Allows sorting of search results on the server rather than on the client. This may be desirable to build simpler, limited function clients.

- The LDAP Application Program Interface

  Defines the C language application program interface (API) to LDAP. Most vendors already incorporate this extension, or at least a subset of it. See Chapter 4, "Building LDAP-Enabled Applications" on page 85, for more information on the C language API.

2.2 The LDAP Models

LDAP can be better understood by considering the four models upon which it is based:

Information   Describes the structure of information stored in an LDAP directory.

Naming   Describes how information in an LDAP directory is organized and identified.

Functional   Describes what operations can be performed on the information stored in an LDAP directory.

Security   Describes how the information in an LDAP directory can be protected from unauthorized access.

The following sections discuss the four LDAP models.

2.2.1 The Information Model

The basic unit of information stored in the directory is called an entry. Entries represent objects of interest in the real world such as people, servers, organizations, and so on. Entries are composed of a collection of attributes that contain information about the object. Every attribute has a type and one or more values. The type of the attribute is associated with a syntax. The syntax specifies what kind of values can be stored. For example, an entry might have a `facsimilieTelephoneNumber` attribute. The syntax associated with this type of attribute would specify that the values are telephone numbers represented as printable strings optionally followed by keywords describing paper size and resolution characteristics. It is possible that the directory entry for an organization would contain multiple values in this attribute—that is that an organization or person represented by the entity would have multiple fax numbers. The relationship between a directory entry and its attributes and their values is shown in Figure 6.

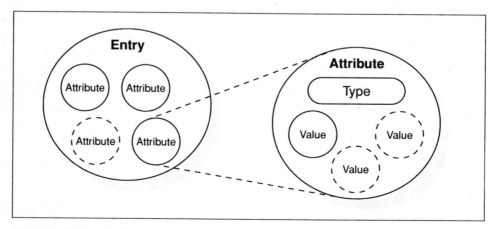

Figure 6. Entries, Attributes and Values

In addition to defining what data can be stored as the value of an attribute, an attribute syntax also defines how those values behave during searches and other directory operations. The attribute `telephoneNumber`, for example, has a syntax that specifies:

- Lexicographic ordering.
- Case, spaces and dashes are ignored during the comparisons.
- Values must be character strings.

For example, using the correct definitions, the telephone numbers "512-838-6008", "512838-6008", and "5128386008" are considered the same. A few of the syntaxes that have been defined for LDAP are listed in the following table.

Table 2. Some of the LDAP Attribute Syntaxes

Syntax	Description
bin	Binary information.
ces	Case exact string, also known as a "directory string", case is significant during comparisons.
cis	Case ignore string. Case is not significant durring comparisons.
tel	Telephone number. The numbers are treated as text, but all blanks and dashes are ignored.
dn	Distinguished name.
Generalized Time	Year, month, day, and time represented as a printable string.
Postal Address	Postal address with lines separated by "$" characters.

Table 3 lists some common attributes. Some attributes have alias names that can be used wherever the full attribute name is used. For example, `cn` can be used when referring to the attribute `commonName`.

Table 3. Common LDAP Attributes

Attribute, Alias	Syntax	Description	Example
commonName, cn	cis	Common name of an entry	John Smith
surname, sn	cis	Surname (last name) of a person	Smith
telephoneNumber	tel	Telephone number	512-838-6008

Attribute, Alias	Syntax	Description	Example
organizationalUnitName, ou	cis	Name of an organizational unit	itso
owner	dn	Distinguished name of the person that owns the entry	cn=John Smith, o=IBM, c=US
organization, o	cis	Name of an organization	IBM
jpegPhoto	bin	Photographic image in JPEG format	Photograph of John Smith

Constraints can be associated with attribute types to limit the number of values that can be stored in the attribute or to limit the total size of a value. For example, an attribute that contains a photo could be limited to a size of 10 KB to prevent the use of unreasonable amounts of storage space. Or an attribute used to store a social security number could be limited to holding a single value.

Schemas define the type of objects that can be stored in the directory. Schemas also list the attributes of each object type and whether these attributes are required or optional. For example, in the person schema, the attribute surname (sn) is required, but the attribute description is optional. Schema-checking ensures that all required attributes for an entry are present before an entry is stored. Schema-checking also ensures that attributes not in the schema are not stored in the entry. Optional attributes can be filled in at any time. Schema also define the inheritance and subclassing of objects and where in the DIT structure (hierarchy) objects may appear.

Table 4 lists a few of the common schema (object classes and their required attributes). In many cases, an entry can consist of more than one object class:

Table 4. Object Classes and Required Attributes

Object Class	Description	Required Attributes
InetOrgPerson	Defines entries for a person	commonName (cn) surname (sn) objectClass
organizationalUnit	Defines entries for organizational units	ou objectClass
organization	Defines entries for organizations	o objectClass

Though each server can define its own schema, for interoperability it is expected that many common schema will be standardized (refer to RFC 2252, *Lightweight Directory Access Protocol (v3): Attribute Syntax Definitions*, and RFC 2256, *A Summary of the X.500(96) User Schema for use with LDAPv3*).

There are times when new schema will be needed at a particular server or within an organization. In LDAP Version 3, a server is required to return information about itself, including the schema that it uses. A program can therefore query a server to determine the contents of the schema. This server information is stored at the special zero-length DN (see 2.2.2, "The Naming Model" on page 28, for more details).

Objects can be derived from other objects. This is known as subclassing. For example, suppose an object called person was defined that included a surname and so on. An object class organizationalPerson could be defined as a subclass of the person object class. The organizationPerson object class would have the same attributes as the person object class and could add other attributes such as `title` and `officenumber`. The person object class would be called the superior of the organizationPerson object class. One special object class, called top, has no superiors. The top object class includes the mandatory `objectClass` attribute. Attributes in top appear in all directory entries as specified (required or optional).

Each directory entry has a special attribute called objectClass. The value of the `objectClass` attribute is a list of two or more schema names. These schema define what type of object(s) the entry represents. One of the values must be either top or alias. Alias is used if the entry is an alias for another entry (see 2.2.2, "The Naming Model" on page 28), otherwise top is used. The `objectClass` attribute determines what attributes the entry must and may have.

The special object class `extensibleObject` allows any attribute to be stored in the entry. This can be more convenient than defining a new object class to add a special attribute to a few entries, but also opens up that object to be able to contain anything (which might not be a good thing in a structured system).

2.2.2 The Naming Model

The LDAP naming model defines how entries are identified and organized. Entries are organized in a tree-like structure called the Directory Information Tree (DIT). Entries are arranged within the DIT based on their distinguished name (DN). A DN is a unique name that unambiguously identifies a single entry. DNs are made up of a sequence of relative distinguished names (RDNs). Each RDN in a DN corresponds to a branch in the DIT leading from the root of the DIT to the directory entry.

Each RDN is derived from the attributes of the directory entry. In the simple and common case, an RDN has the form <attribute name> = <value> (see Figure 8 on page 31 for the complete syntax of DNs and RDNs). A DN is composed of a sequence of RDNs separated by commas.

An example of a DIT is shown in Figure 7. The example is very simple, but can be used to illustrate some basic concepts. Each box represents a directory entry. The root directory entry is conceptual, but does not actually exist. Attributes are listed inside each entry. The list of attributes shown is not complete. For example, the entry for the country DE (c=DE) could have an attribute called description with the value Germany.

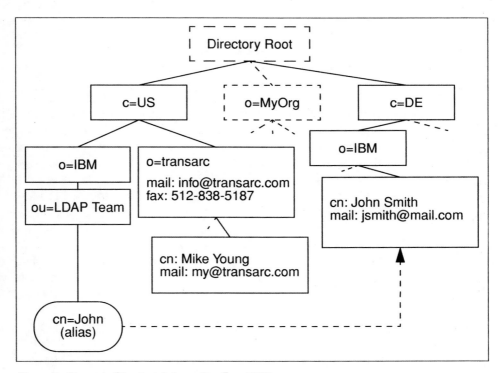

Figure 7. Example Directory Information Tree (DIT)

The organization of the entries in the DIT are restricted by their corresponding object class definitions. It is usual to follow either a geographical or an organizational scheme. For example, entries that represent countries would be at the top of the DIT. Below the countries would be national organizations, states, and provinces, and so on. Below this level, entries might represent people within those organizations or further subdivisions of the organization. The lowest layers of the DIT entries could represent any object, such as people, printers, application servers, and so on. The depth or breadth of the DIT is not restricted and can be designed to suit application requirements. See Chapter 3, "Designing and Maintaining an LDAP Directory" on page 57, for information on designing a DIT.

Entries are named according to their position in the DIT. The directory entry in the lower-right corner of Figure 7 has the DN `cn=John Smith,o=IBM,c=DE`. Note that DNs read from leaf to root as opposed to file system names which usually read from root to leaf. The DN is made up of a sequence of RDNs. Each RDN is constructed from an attribute (or attributes) of the entry it names. For example, the DN `cn=John Smith,o=IBM,c=DE` is constructed by adding the RDN `cn=John Smith` to the DN of the ancestor entry `o=IBM,c=DE`. Note that `cn=John Smith` is an attribute in the entry `cn=John Smith,o=IBM,c=DE`. The DN of an entry is specified when it is created. It would have been legal, though not intuitive, to have created the entry with the DN `mail=jsmith@mail.com,o=IBM,c=DE`.

The DIT is described as being tree-like implying it is not a tree. This is because of aliases. Aliases allow the tree structure to be circumvented. This can be useful if an entry belongs to more than one organization or if a commonly used DN is too complex. Another common use of aliases is when entries are moved within the DIT and you want access to continue to work as before. In Figure 7, `cn=John,ou=LDAP Team,o=IBM,c=US` is an alias for `cn=John Smith,o=IBM,c=DE`. Aliases do not have to point to leaf entries in the DIT. For example, `o=Redbook,c=US` could be an alias for `ou=ITSO,o=IBM,c=US`.

2.2.2.1 Distinguished Name Syntax

DNs are used as primary keys to entries in the directory. LDAP defines a user-oriented string representation of DNs. The syntax of DNs, which consist of a sequence of RDNs, was described informally above. Figure 8 on page 31 shows the formal grammar of DNs.

Note that RDNs can be more complicated than in the examples shown above. An RDN can be composed of multiple attributes joined by "+" as in the DN `cn=John Smith+l=Stuttgart,o=IBM,c=DE`.

If attribute values contain special characters or leading or trailing spaces, those characters must be escaped by preceding them with a backslash character. The following DN contains a comma character `o=Transarc\, Inc.,c=US`.

DNs in LDAP Version 3 are more restrictive than in LDAP V2. For example, in LDAP V2, semicolons could also be used to separate RDNs. LDAP V3 must accept the older syntax, but must not generate DNs that do not conform to the newer syntax. The exact grammar for a distinguished name syntax is shown in Figure 8.

```
distinguishedName = [name]                        ; may be empty string

name       = name-component *("," name-component)

name-component = attributeTypeAndValue *("+" attributeTypeAndValue)

attributeTypeAndValue = attributeType "=" attributeValue

attributeType = (ALPHA 1*keychar) / oid
keychar    = ALPHA / DIGIT / "-"

oid        = 1*DIGIT *("." 1*DIGIT)

attributeValue = string

string     = *( stringchar / pair )
             / "#" hexstring
             / QUOTATION *( quotechar / pair ) QUOTATION ; only from v2

quotechar    = <any character except "\" or QUOTATION >

special    = "," / "=" / "+" / "<" /  ">" / "#" / ";"

pair       = "\" ( special / "\" / QUOTATION / hexpair )
stringchar = <any character except one of special, "\" or QUOTATION >

hexstring  = 1*hexpair
hexpair    = hexchar hexchar

hexchar    = DIGIT / "A" / "B" / "C" / "D" / "E" / "F"
             / "a" / "b" / "c" / "d" / "e" / "f"

ALPHA      = <any ASCII alphabetic character>      ; (decimal 65-90 and 97-122)
DIGIT      = <any ASCII decimal digit>             ; (decimal 48-57)
QUOTATION  = <the ASCII double quotation mark character '"' decimal 34>
```

Figure 8. Distinguished Name Grammar

The attribute types used in the RDN can be represented by a dotted decimal string encoding of its object identifier. For example, cn=John could also be written as 2.5.4.2=John. However, frequently used attribute names have a string representation that is obviously easier to understand. Table 5 lists some of the common attribute types and their string representation. Please notice that because attribute names are case insensitive, you might see different uppercase/lowercase notations in the literature.

Table 5. Attribute Type String Representations

Attribute Type	String
CommonName	CN
LocalityName	L
StateOrProvinceName	ST
OrganizationName	O
OrganizationalUnitName	OU
CountryName	C
StreetAddress	STREET
domainComponent	DC
userid	UID

2.2.2.2 Suffixes and Referrals

An individual LDAP server might not store the entire DIT. A server might store the entries for a particular department and not the entries for the ancestors of the department. For example, a server might store the entries for the ITSO department at IBM. The highest node in the DIT stored by the server would be ou=ITSO, o=IBM, c=US. The server would not store entries for c=US or for o=IBM, c=US. The highest entry stored by a server is called a suffix. Each entry stored by the server ends with this suffix (remember that in the DN syntax, the higher-level entries are at the end).

A server can support multiple suffixes. For example, in addition to storing information about the ITSO department, the same server could store information about the sales department at Transarc. The server would then have the suffixes ou=ITSO, o=IBM, c=US and ou=sales, o=Transarc, c=US.

Since a server might not store the entire DIT, servers need to be linked together in some way in order to form a distributed directory that contains the entire DIT. This is accomplished with referrals. Continuing the example, another server might store the entry o=IBM, c=US but not information about the ITSO department. If somebody searched this directory server for information about the ITSO department, no information would be found. However, the server can store a referral to the LDAP server that does contain the information. This referral acts like a pointer that can be followed to where the desired information is stored. Such an example is shown in Figure 9, where the referral arrow shows the logical connection of a referral and does not reflect the technical implementaion (see text that follows).

A referral is an entry of `objectClass` referral. It has an attribute, `ref`, whose value is the LDAP URL of the referred entry on another LDAP server. See 4.4, "LDAP URLs" on page 120, for information about LDAP URLs.

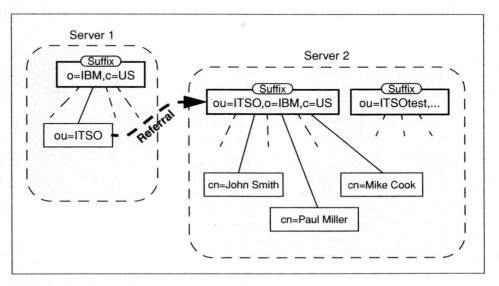

Figure 9. Example DIT Showing Suffixes and Referrals

When a client sends a request to an LDAP server, the response to the client may be a referral. The client can then choose to follow the referral by querying the other LDAP server contained in the referral returned by the first LDAP server. Referrals are not followed (resolved) by servers. This can improve server performance by off-loading the work of contacting other servers to the client.

Figure 10 illustrates a client following a referral. An LDAP client requests information from LDAP Server 1 (1). This request is answered with a referral to LDAP Server 2 (2). The LDAP client then contacts LDAP Server 2 (3). LDAP Server 2 provides the requested data to the client (4).

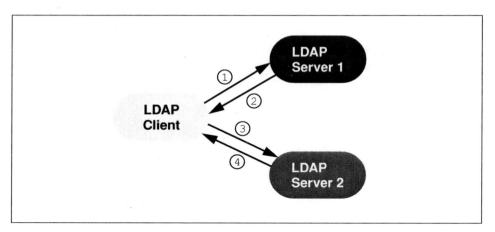

Figure 10. Referral Followed by Client

Figure 11 illustrates chaining. An LDAP client requests information from
LDAP Server 1 (1). LDAP Server 1 finds a referral to Server 2 and forwards
the request (2). Server 2 provides the requested data to LDAP Server 1 (3).
LDAP Server 1 then returns the result to the client (4). Note that this
explanation and Figure 11 are for illustration purposes only since chaining is
not included in either the LDAP Version 2 or Version 3 specifications.

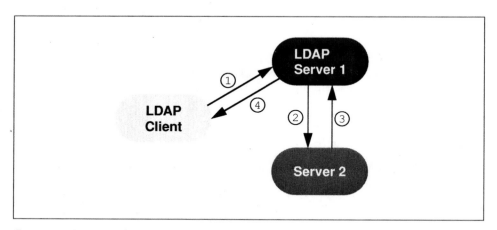

Figure 11. Server Chaining

The LDAP API allows the programmer to specify whether returned referrals
should be followed automatically or returned to the program. If referrals are
followed automatically, the LDAP client library (not the server nor the
application program) follows the referral. This requires no extra coding and is
transparent to the programmer. To prevent lengthy searches or referrals that

(mistakenly) form a loop, the programmer can limit the number of referrals followed for a request.

If the referral is returned to the program, code must be supplied to recognize that a referral has been returned. The referral can be examined and a decision made whether to follow it or not. This is more complicated, but gives the programmer greater choice of which referrals to follow.

Referrals allow a DIT to be partitioned and distributed across multiple servers. Portions of the DIT can also be replicated. This can improve performance and availability. See Chapter 3, "Designing and Maintaining an LDAP Directory" on page 57, for information on designing a distributed directory.

LDAP Version 2 did not formally define referrals, but Version 3 does include them. Neither Version 2 nor Version 3 define chaining, but it is not prohibited if vendors chose to implement it. Vendors, for example, may chose to implement an X.500-type chaining mechanism or functionality provided by distributed databases to achieve this.

2.2.2.3 Server Information

An LDAP Version 3 server must provide information about itself. The special entry called the root DSE with a zero-length (empty) DN contains attributes that describe the server. These attributes can be retrieved to discover basic information about the server and the DIT that it stores. Server-specific information available includes:

- The suffixes, also called naming contexts, the server stores
- The DN of a special entry that contains a list of all the objectClass and attribute schema known to the server
- The version(s) of LDAP supported,
- A list of supported extended operations and controls (see 2.2.3.7, "Controls and Extended Operations" on page 41)
- A list of supported SASL security mechanisms
- A list of alternate LDAP servers

As LDAP is extended, additional information about the server will be stored in the root DSE.

2.2.3 The Functional Model

LDAP defines operations for accessing and modifying directory entries. This section discusses LDAP operations in a programming language-independent manner. See Chapter 4, "Building LDAP-Enabled Applications" on page 85, for information on writing programs that invoke these operations.

LDAP operations can be divided into the following three categories:

Query   Includes the search and compare operations used to retrieve information from a directory

Update   Includes the add, delete, modify, and modify RDN operations used to update stored information in a directory

Authentication Includes the bind, unbind, and abandon operations used to connect and disconnect to and from an LDAP server, establish access rights and protect information

The most common operation is search. The search operation is very flexible and has some of the most complex options.

2.2.3.1 Search

The search operation allows a client to request that an LDAP server search through some portion of the DIT for information meeting user-specified criteria in order to read and list the result(s). There are no separate operations for read and list; they are incorporated in the search function. The search can be very general or very specific. The search operation allows one to specify the starting point within the DIT, how deep within the DIT to search, what attributes an entry must have to be considered a match, and what attributes to return for matched entries.

Some example searches expressed informally in English are:

- Find the postal address for cn=John Smith, o=IBM, c=DE.

- Find all the entries that are children of the entry ou=ITSO, o=IBM, c=US.

- Find the e-mail address and phone number of anyone in IBM whose last name contains the characters "miller" and who also has a fax number.

To perform a search, the following parameters must be specified (refer to Figure 12 on page 38):

- Base

  A DN that defines the starting point, called the base object, of the search. The base object is a node within the DIT.

- Scope

  Specifies how deep within the DIT to search from the base object. There are three choices: baseObject, singleLevel, and wholeSubtree. If baseObject is specified, only the base object is examined. If singleLevel is specified, only the immediate children of the base object are examined; the base object itself is not examined. If `wholeSubtree` is specified, the base object and all of its descendants are examined.

- Search Filter

  Specifies the criteria an entry must match to be returned from a search. The search filter is a Boolean combination of attribute value assertions. An attribute value assertion tests the value of an attribute for equality, less than or equal, and so on. For example, a search filter might specify entries with a common name containing "wolf" or belonging to the organization ITSO. Search filters are discussed more fully in 2.2.3.3, "Search Filter Syntax" on page 39.

- Attributes to Return

  Specifies which attributes to retrieve from entries that match the search criteria. Since an entry may have many attributes, this allows the user to only see the attributes they are interested in. Normally, the user is interested in the value of the attributes. However, it is possible to return only the attribute types and not their values. This could be useful if a large value like a JPEG photograph was not needed for every entry returned from the search, but some of the photographs would be retrieved later as needed.

- Alias Dereferencing

  Specifies if aliases are dereferenced—that is, if the alias entry itself or the entry it points to is used. Aliases can be dereferenced or not when locating the base object and/or when searching under the base object. If aliases are dereferenced, then they are alternate names for objects of interest in the directory. Not dereferencing aliases allows the alias entries themselves to be examined.

- Limits

  Searches can be very general, examining large subtrees and causing many entries to be returned. The user can specify time and size limits to prevent wayward searching from consuming too many resources. The size limit restricts the number of entries returned from the search. The time limit limits the total time of the search. Servers are free to impose stricter limits than requested by the client.

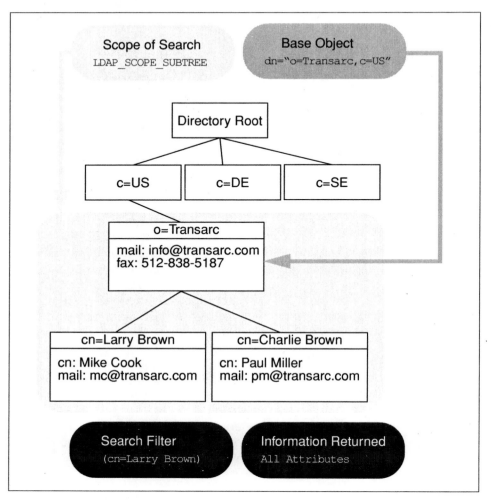

Figure 12. Search Parameters

2.2.3.2 Referrals and Continuation References

If the server does not contain the base object, it will return a referral to a server that does, if possible. Once the base object is found `singleLevel` and `wholeSubtree` searches may encounter other referrals. These referrals are returned in the search result along with other matching entries. These referrals are called continuation references because they indicate where a search could be continued.

For example, when searching a subtree for anybody named Smith, a continuation reference to another server might be returned, possibly along with several other matching entries. It is not guaranteed that an entry for somebody named Smith actually exists at that server, only that the continuation reference points to a subtree that could contain such an entry. It is up to the client to follow continuation references if desired.

Since only LDAP Version 3 specifies referrals, continuation references are not supported in earlier versions.

2.2.3.3 Search Filter Syntax

The search filter defines criteria that an entry must match to be returned from a search. The basic component of a search filter is an attribute value assertion of the form:

```
attribute operator value
```

For example, to search for a person named John Smith the search filter would be `cn=John Smith`. In this case, `cn` is the attribute; `=` is the operator, and `John Smith` is the value. This search filter matches entries with the common name John Smith.

Table 6 lists the operators for search filters.

Table 6. Search Filter Operators

Operator	Description	Example
=	Returns entries whose attribute is equal to the value.	`cn=John Smith` finds the entry with common name John Smith
>=	Returns entries whose attribute is greater than or equal to the value.	`sn>=smith` finds all entries from smith to z*
<=	Returns entries whose attribute is less than or equal to the value.	`sn<=smith` finds all entries from a* to `smith`
=*	Returns entries that have a value set for that attribute.	`sn=*` finds all entries that have the `sn` attribute
~=	Returns entries whose attribute value approximately matches the specified value. Typically, this is an algorithm that matches words that sound alike.	`sn~= smit` might find the entry "`sn=smith`"

The "*" character matches any substring and can be used with the = operator. For example, `cn=J*Smi*` would match John Smith and Jan Smitty.

Search filters can be combined with Boolean operators to form more complex search filters. The syntax for combining search filters is:

```
( "&" or "|" (filter1) (filter2) (filter3) ...)
("!" (filter))
```

The Boolean operators are listed in Table 7.

Table 7. Boolean Operators

Boolean Operator	Description
&	Returns entries matching all specified filter criteria.
|	Returns entries matching one or more of the filter criteria.
!	Returns entries for which the filter is not true. This operator can only be applied to a single filter. `(!(filter))` is valid, but `(!(filter1)(filter2))` is not.

For example, `(|(sn=Smith)(sn=Miller))` matches entries with the surname Smith or the surname Miller. The Boolean operators can also be nested as in `(| (sn=Smith) (&(ou=Austin)(sn=Miller)))`, which matches any entry with the surname Smith or with the surname Miller that also has the organizational unit attribute Austin.

2.2.3.4 Compare

The compare operation compares an entry for an attribute value. If the entry has that value, compare returns TRUE. Otherwise, compare returns FALSE. Although compare is simpler than a search, it is almost the same as a base scope search with a search filter of attribute=value. The difference is that if the entry does not have the attribute at all (the attribute is not present), the search will return not found. This is indistinguishable from the case where the entry itself does not exist. On the other hand, compare will return FALSE. This indicates that the entry does exist, but does not have an attribute matching the value specified.

2.2.3.5 Update Operations

Update operations modify the contents of the directory. Table 8 summarizes the update operations.

Table 8. Update Operations

Operation	Description
add	Inserts new entries into the directory.
delete	Deletes existing entries from the directory. Only leaf nodes can be deleted. Aliases are not resolved when deleting.

Operation	Description
modify	Changes the attributes and values contained within an existing entry. Allows new attributes to be added and existing attributes to be deleted or modified.
modify DN	Change the least significant (left most) component of a DN or moves a subtree of entries to a new location in the DIT. Entries cannot be moved across server boundaries.

2.2.3.6 Authentication Operations

Authentication operations are used to establish and end a session between an LDAP client and an LDAP server. The session may be secured at various levels ranging from an insecure anonymous session, an authenticated session in which the client identifies itself by providing a password, to a secure, encrypted session using SASL mechanisms. SASL was added in LDAP Version 3 to overcome the weak authentication in LDAP Version 2 (some vendors, however, have added stronger authentication methods, such as Kerberos, to LDAP Version 2). Table 9 summarizes the authentication operations. The security aspects are discussed further in 2.2.4, "The Security Model" on page 42 and in 2.3, "Security" on page 43.

Table 9. Authentication Operations

Operation	Description
Bind	Initiates an LDAP session between a client and a server. Allows the client to prove its identity by authenticating itself to the server.
Unbind	Terminates a client/server session.
Abandon	Allows a client to request that the server abandon an outstanding operation.

2.2.3.7 Controls and Extended Operations

Controls and extended operations allow the LDAP protocol to be extended without changing the protocol itself. Controls modify the behavior of an operation, and extended operations add new operations to the LDAP protocol. The list of controls and extensions supported by an LDAP server can be obtained by examining the empty DN at that server (see 2.2.2.3, "Server Information" on page 35).

Controls can be defined to extend any operation. Controls are added to the end of the operation's protocol message. They are supplied as parameters to functions in the API. In the future, standard controls might be defined in LDAP-related RFCs.

A control has a dotted decimal string object ID used to identify the control, an arbitrary control value that holds parameters for the control, and a criticality level. If the criticality level is TRUE, the server must honor the control or if the server does not support the control, reject the entire operation. If the criticality level is FALSE, a server that does not support the control must perform the operation as if there was no control specified.

For example, a control might extend the delete operation by causing an audit record of the deletion to be logged to a file specified by the control value information.

An extended operation allows an entirely new operation to be defined. The extended operation protocol message consists of a dotted decimal string object ID used to identify the extended operation and an arbitrary string of operation-specific data.

2.2.4 The Security Model

As previously described, the security model is based on the bind operation. There are several different bind operations possible, and thus the security mechanism applied is different as well. One possibility is when a client requesting access supplies a DN identifying itself along with a simple clear-text password. If no DN and password is declared, an anonymous session is assumed by the LDAP server. The use of clear text passwords is strongly discouraged when the underlying transport service cannot guarantee confidentiality and may therefore result in disclosure of the password to unauthorized parties.

Additionally, a Kerberos bind is possible in LDAP Version 2, but this has become deprecated in LDAP Version 3. Instead, LDAP V3 comes along with a bind command supporting the Simple Authentication and Security Layer (SASL) mechanism. This is a general authentication framework, where several different authentication methods are available for authenticating the client to the server; one of them is Kerberos. We discuss authentication in more detail in the following section 2.3, "Security" on page 43.

Furthermore, extended protocol operations are available in LDAP V3. An extension related to security is the "Extension for Transport Layer Security (TLS) for LDAPv3" which, at the time this book was written, is an Internet Draft (see A.4, "Other Sources" on page 140 for an URL). It defines operations that use TLS as a means to encrypt an LDAP session and protect it against spoofing. TLS is defined in "The TLS Protocol" Version 1.0, which is also still an Internet Draft. It is based on the Secure Socket Layer (SSL) Protocol 3.0, devised by Netscape Communications Corporation which it eventually will supersede. TLS has a mechanism which enables it to communicate to an SSL server so that it is backwards compatible. The basic principles of SSL and TLS are the same and are further detailed in the following section 2.3, "Security" on page 43.

Some vendors, like Netscape and IBM, have already extended the LDAP protocol and added some SSL specific commands so that an encrypted TCP/IP connection is possible, thus providing a means for eliminating the need of sending a DN and a password unprotected over the network

Once a client is identified, access control information can be consulted to determine whether or not the client has sufficient access permissions to do what it is requesting.

2.3 Security

Security is of great importance in the networked world of computers, and this is true for LDAP as well. When sending data over insecure networks, internally or externally, sensitive information may need to be protected during transportation. There is also a need to know who is requesting the information and who is sending it. This is especially important when it comes to the update operations on a directory. The term security, as used in the context of this book, generally covers the following four aspects:

Authentication   Assurance that the opposite party (machine or person) really is who he/she/it claims to be.

Integrity   Assurance that the information that arrives is really the same as what was sent.

Confidentiality   Protection of information disclosure by means of data encryption to those who are not intended to receive it.

Authorization   Assurance that a party is really allowed to do what he/she/it is requesting to do. This is usually checked after user authentication. In LDAP Version 3, this is currently not part of the protocol specification and is therefore implementation- (or vendor-) specific. This is basically achieved by assigning access controls, like read, write, or delete, to user IDs or common names. There is an Internet Draft that proposes access control for LDAP.

The following sections focus on the first three aspects (since authorization is not contained in the LDAP Version 3 standard): authentication, integrity and confidentiality. There are several methods that can be used for this purpose; the most important ones are discussed here. These are:

- No authentication
- Basic authentication
- Simple Authentication and Security Layer (SASL)

Because no other data encryption method was available in LDAP Version 2, some vendors, for example Netscape and IBM, added their own SSL calls to the LDAP API. A potential drawback of such an approach is that the API calls might not be compatible among different vendor implementations. Therefore, in LDAP Version 3, a proposal is made (Extension for Transport Layer Security) to include SSL or, more accurately, its successor, TLS, through extended protocol operations. This should make the vendor-dependent functions redundant in the near future.

2.3.1 No Authentication

This is the simplest way, one that obviously does not need to be explained in much detail. This method should only be used when data security is not an issue and when no special access control permissions are involved. This could be the case, for example, when your directory is an address book browsable by anybody. No authentication is assumed when you leave the password and DN field empty in the bind API call (see also Chapter 4, "Building LDAP-Enabled Applications" on page 85). The LDAP server then automatically assumes an anonymous user session and grants access with the appropriate access controls defined for this kind of access (not to be confused with the SASL anonymous user as discussed in 2.3.3, "Simple Authentication and Security Layer (SASL)" on page 45).

2.3.2 Basic Authentication

The security mechanism in LDAP is negotiated when the connection between the client and the server is established. This is the approach specified in the LDAP application program interface (API). Beside the option of using no authentication at all, the most simple security mechanism in LDAP is called basic authentication, which is also used in several other Web-related protocols, such as in HTTP.

When using basic authentication with LDAP, the client identifies itself to the server by means of a DN and a password which are sent in the clear over the network (some implementation may use Base64 encoding instead). The server considers the client authenticated if the DN and password sent by the client matches the password for that DN stored in the directory. Base64 encoding is defined in the Multipurpose Internet Mail Extensions (MIME) standard (RFC 1521). It is a relatively simple encryption, and therefore it is not hard to break once one has captured the data on the network.

2.3.3 Simple Authentication and Security Layer (SASL)

SASL is a framework for adding additional authentication mechanisms to connection-oriented protocols. It has been added to LDAP Version 3 to overcome the authentication shortcomings of Version 2. SASL was originally devised to add stronger authentication to the IMAP protocol. SASL has since evolved into a more general system for mediating between protocols and authentication systems. It is a proposed Internet standard defined in RFC 2222.

In SASL, connection protocols, like LDAP, IMAP, and so on, are represented by profiles; each profile is considered a protocol extension that allows the protocol and SASL to work together. A complete list of SASL profiles can be obtained from the Information Sciences Institute (ISI). See A.4, "Other Sources" on page 140, for URL references. Among these are IMAP4, SMTP, POP3, and LDAP. Each protocol that intends to use SASL needs to be extended with a command to identify an authentication mechanism and to carry out an authentication exchange. Optionally, a security layer can be negotiated to encrypt the data after authentication and so ensure confidentiality. LDAP Version 3 includes such a command (`ldap_sasl_bind()`).

The SASL bind operation is explained in more detail with an example in 4.2.8, "Authentication Methods" on page 108. The key parameters that influence the security method used are:

dn   This is the distinguished name of the entry you want to bind as.
             This can be thought of as the user ID in a normal user ID and
             password authentication.

mechanism   This is the name of the security method that should be used.
             Valid security mechanisms are currently Kerberos Version 4,
             S/Key, GSSAPI, CRAM-MD5 and EXTERNAL. There is also an
             ANONYMOUS mechanism available which enables an
             authentication as user "anonymous". In LDAP, the most common
             mechanism used is SSL (or its successor, TLS), which is
             provided as an EXTERNAL mechanism.

credentials This contains the arbitrary data that identifies the DN. The
             format and content of the parameter depends on the mechanism
             chosen. If it is, for example, the ANONYMOUS mechanism, it
             can be an arbitrary string or an e-mail address that identifies the
             user.

Through the SASL bind API function call, LDAP client applications call the
SASL protocol driver on the server, which in turn connects the authentication
system named in the SASL mechanism to retrieve the required authentication
information for the user. SASL can be seen as intermediator between the
authentication system and a protocol like LDAP. Figure 13 illustrates this
relationship.

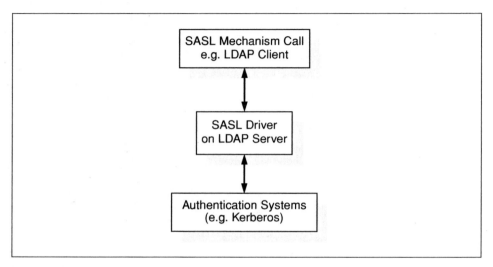

Figure 13. SASL Mechanism

Of course, the server must support this SASL mechanism as well, otherwise
the authentication process will not be able to succeed. To retrieve a list of
SASL mechanisms supported by an LDAP server (Version 3 only), point your
Web browser to the following URL:

```
ldap://<ldap server>/?supportedsaslmechanisms
```

This is actually an LDAP URL, very similar to those used for HTTP
(`http://<host>/...`) or other Internet protocols. You can get more information
about LDAP URLs in 4.4, "LDAP URLs" on page 120.

As we have seen, the basic idea behind SASL is that it provides a high level
framework that lets the involved parties decide on the particular security
mechanism to use. The SASL security mechanism negotiation between client
and server is done in the clear. Once the client and the server have agreed on
a common mechanism, the connection is secure against modifying the
authentication identities. An attacker could now try to eavesdrop the
mechanism negotiation and cause a party to use the least secure
mechanism. In order to prevent this from happening, clients and servers

should be configured to use a minimum security mechanism, provided they support such a configuration option.

As stated earlier, SSL and its successor, TLS, are the mechanisms commonly used in SASL for LDAP. Following is a brief description of SSL and TLS.

2.3.3.1 SSL and TLS

The Secure Socket Layer (SSL) protocol was devised to provide both authentication and data security. It encapsulates the TCP/IP socket so that basically every TCP/IP application can use it to secure its communication. See Figure 14.

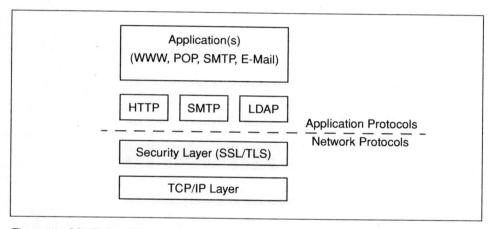

Figure 14. SSL/TLS in Relationship with Other Protocols

SSL was developed by Netscape and the current version is 3.0. Transport Layer Security (TLS) is an evolving open standard, currently in the state of an Internet Draft, being worked on at the IETF. It is based on SSL 3.0 with only a few minor differences, and it provides backwards compatibility with SSL 3.0. It is assumed that TLS will replace SSL. The following discussion is equally valid for both SSL and TLS.

SSL/TLS supports server authentication (client authenticates server), client authentication (server authenticates client), or mutual authentication. In addition, it provides for privacy by encrypting data sent over the network.

SSL/TLS uses a public key method to secure the communication and to authenticate the counterparts of the session. This is achieved with a public/private key pair. They operate as reverse functions to each other, which means data encrypted with the private key can be decrypted with the public key and vice versa. The assumption for the following considerations is that the server has its key pair already generated. This is usually done when setting up the LDAP server.

The simplified interchange between a client and a server negotiating an SSL/TLS connection is explained in the following segment and illustrated in Figure 15.

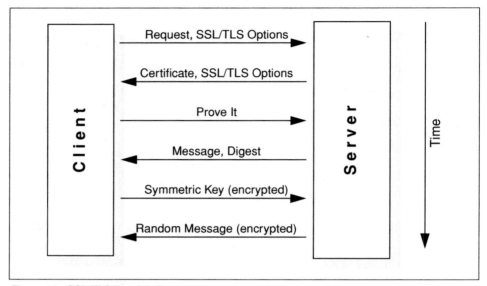

Figure 15. SSL/TLS Handshake

1. As a first step, the client asks the server for an SSL/TLS session. The client also includes the SSL/TLS options it supports in the request.

2. The server sends back its SSL/TLS options and a certificate which includes, among other things, the server's public key, the identity for whom the certificate was issued (as a distinguished name), the certifier's name and the validity time. A certificate can be thought of the electronic equivalent of a passport. It has to be issued by a general, trusted Certificate Authority (CA) which vouches that the public key really belongs to the entity mentioned in the certificate. The certificate is signed by the certifier which can be verified with the certifier's freely available public key

3. The client then requests the server to prove its identity. This is to make sure that the certificate was not sent by someone else who intercepted it on a former occasion.

4. The server sends back a message including a message digest (similar to a check sum) which is encrypted with its private key. A message digest that is computed from the message content using a hash function has two

features. It is extremely difficult to reverse, and it is nearly impossible to find a message that would produce the same digest. The client can decrypt the digest with the server's public key and then compare it with the digest it computes from the message. If both are equal, the server's identity is proved, and the authentication process is finished.

5. Next, server and client have to agree upon a secret (symmetric) key used for data encryption. Data encryption is done with a symmetric key algorithm because it is more efficient than the computing-intensive public key method. The client therefore generates a symmetric key, encrypts it with the server's public key, and sends it to the server. Only the server with its private key can decrypt the secret key.

6. The server decrypts the secret key and sends back a test message encrypted with the secret key to prove that the key has safely arrived. They can now start communicating using the symmetric key to encrypt the data.

As outlined above, SSL/TLS is used to authenticate a server to a client using its certificate and its private key and to negotiate a secret key later on used for data encryption. An example on how SSL can be used in a client application can be found in 4.2.8, "Authentication Methods" on page 108.

2.3.3.2 Other SASL Authentication Mechanisms

Although the SASL concepts supports multiple mechanisms, a particular vendor product may not support them all. It is very likely that vendor products only support a few mechanisms, such as SSL or TLS as just discussed above. Another common authentication method widely used is Kerberos. It has its roots in universities, where it proved to be scalable up to many thousands of clients. Kerberos is a third-party authentication method that uses a separate server providing security functions for the authentication process between involved parties. It uses the widely accepted Data Encryption Standard (DES) for message encryption.

2.4 Manageability

The LDAP specifications contained in the pertinent RFCs (as listed and briefly explained in 2.1, "Overview of LDAP Architecture" on page 19) include functions for directory data management. These include functions to create and modify the directory information tree (DIT) and to add, modify, and delete data stored in the directory.

Vendor products, however, most likely include additional tools that allow you to configure and manage an LDAP server environment. These may be command line based or graphical applications that include functions like:

- Server setup (initial creation)
- Configuring a directory information tree
- Contents management
- Security setup
- Replication and referrals management
- Access control management
- Logging and log file management
- Resource management and performance analysis tools

In B.3, "Tivoli User Administration: LDAP Endpoint" on page 147 we describe a product-independent management tool that provides the administration functions for users in an LDAP directory service.

Despite of the lack of comprehensive management tools in the standards, there are some basic but powerful mechanisms in LDAP that are important to know, as described in the following sections.

2.4.1 LDAP Command Line Tools

Most LDAP Software Development Kits (SDKs) provide a set of easy-to-use client command line applications that can do the basic LDAP protocol operations like search the directory, or add, modify, delete, or rename entries. These tools are also capable of reading their data from LDIF files (see following section) so that they can be used to manage bulk directory data. They can conveniently be used within other command language programs, such as UNIX shell scripts or Perl, to perform daily operations tailored to individual requirements. Because they are often used in development environments, they are described in more details in 4.3, "LDAP Command Line Tools" on page 115.

2.4.2 LDAP Data Interchange Format (LDIF)

When an LDAP directory is loaded for the first time or when many entries have to be changed at once, it is not very convenient to change every single entry on a one-by-one basis. For this purpose, LDAP supports the LDAP Data Interchange Format (LDIF) that can be seen as a convenient, yet necessary, data management mechanism. It enables easy manipulation of mass amounts of data. LDIF is currently defined in an Internet Draft.

LDIF is typically used to import and export directory information between LDAP-based directory servers, for example when an LDAP server has to be moved to other hardware or to describe a set of changes that are to be applied to a directory.

Additionally, by using a well-defined interchange format, development of data import tools from legacy systems is facilitated. Simple tools can be developed, for example using the UNIX shell script language, to convert a database of personnel information into an LDIF file, which can then in turn be imported into the LDAP directory, regardless of the internal database representation the target directory server uses.

2.4.2.1 The LDIF File Format

The LDIF format is used to convey directory information or a description of a set of changes made to directory entries. An LDIF file consists of a series of records separated by line separators. A record consists of a sequence of lines describing a directory entry or a sequence of lines describing a set of changes to a single directory entry. An LDIF file specifies a set of directory entries or a set of changes to be applied to directory entries, but not both at the same time.

The basic form of a directory entry represented in LDIF is:

```
[<id>]
dn: <distinguished name>
objectClass: <object class>
objectClass: <object class>
...
<attribute type>[;language tag]:<attribute value>
<attribute type>[;language tag]:<attribute value>
...
```

Only the DN and at least one object class definition are required. In addition, any attributes required by the object classes for the entry must also be defined in the entry. All other attributes and object classes are optional. You can specify object classes and attributes in any order. The space character after the colon is optional.

Table 10 describes the LDIF fields shown in the previous definition of a directory entry in an LDIF file.

Table 10. Description of LDIF Fields

Field	Definition
[<id>]	An optional positive decimal number representing the entry ID. The database creation tools generate this ID.
dn: <distinguished name>	Specifies the distinguished name for the entry.
objectClass: <object class>	Specifies an object class to use with this entry. The object class identifies the types of attributes, or schema, allowed and required for the entry.
<attribute type>	Specifies a descriptive attribute type to use with the entry.
language tag	Specifies the language of the text in the attribute value.
<attribute value>	Specifies the attribute value to be used with the attribute type.

More details about distinguished names and attributes can be found in 2.2.1, "The Information Model" on page 25, and in 2.2.2, "The Naming Model" on page 28.

2.4.2.2 Data Encoding

Binary data, such as a JPEG image, can be represented in LDIF by using Base64 encoding. Base64 encoded data is identified by using the double-colon (::) symbol, as in the following example:

```
jpegPhoto:: <encoded data>
```

In addition to binary data, other values that must be Base64 encoded include:

- Any value that begins with a semi-colon (;) or a space
- Any value that contains non-ASCII data

Character encoding in LDIF should be in compliance with the UTF-8 standard.

2.4.2.3 Creating Directory Entries Using LDIF

There are many types of entries that can be stored in a directory. This section will show three of the most common types of entries used in a directory: organization, organizational unit, and organizational person entries.

The object classes defined for an entry are what indicates whether the entry represents an organization, an organizational unit, an organizational person, or something else entirely different from these types of entries.

Specifying Organization Entries

Most directories have at least one organization entry. Typically, this is the first, or root, or topmost entry in the directory. The organization entry often corresponds to the suffix set for the directory. That is, if the directory is defined to use a suffix of o=ibm.com, then the organization will probably have an entry in the directory named o=ibm.com. For more information on choosing suffixes, see 3.1.1, "Defining the Data Model" on page 58.

The LDIF entry that is specified to define an organization entry should appear as follows:

```
dn: <distinguished name>
objectClass: top
objectClass: organization
o: <organization name>
<list of optional attributes>
...
```

Table 11 describes the fields:

Table 11. LDIF Fields for Specifying Organization Entries

Field	Definition
dn: <distinguished name>	Specifies the DN for the entry. A DN is required.
objectClass: top	Specifies the top object class. This object class specification is optional. Some older LDAP clients require the existence of object class top during search operations.
objectClass: organization	Specifies the organization object class. This line defines the entry as an organization.
o: <organization name>	Attribute that specifies the organization's name.
<list of attributes>	Specifies the list of optional attributes for the entry.

The following is a sample organization entry in LDIF format:

```
dn: o=ibm.com
objectclass: top
objectclass: organization
```

```
o: ibm.com
telephonenumber: 838-6004
```

Specifying Organizational Unit Entries

There may be more than one organizational unit, or branch point, within a directory tree. For information on how to design a directory tree, see 3.1, "Directory Design Guidelines" on page 57.

The LDIF that you specify to define an organizational unit entry should appear as follows:

```
dn: <distinguished name>
objectClass: top
objectClass: organizationalUnit
ou: <organizational unit name>
<list of optional attributes>
...
```

Table 12 lists and explains the fields:

Table 12. LDIF Fields for Specifying an Organizational Unit

Field	Definition
objectClass: organizationalUnit	Specifies the organizationalUnit object class. This line defines the entry as an organizational unit.
ou: <organizational unit name>	Attribute that specifies the organizational unit's name.

The following is an example organizational unit entry in LDIF format:

```
dn: ou=people, o=ibm.com
objectclass: top
objectclass: organizationalUnit
ou: people
```

Specifying Organizational Person Entries

A common type of entry that will be included in directories will describe a person within the organization. The majority of the entries in the directory will represent organizational people.

The LDIF used to define an organizational person should appear as follows:

```
dn: <distinguished name>
objectClass: top
objectClass: person
objectClass: organizationalPerson
cn: <common name>
```

```
sn: <surname>
<list of optional attributes>
...
```

Table 13 explains the fields:

Table 13. LDIF Fields for Specifying an Organizational Unit

Field	Definition
`objectClass: person`	Specifies the person object class. This object class specification should be included because many LDAP clients will require the existence of object class person during search operations for a person or an organizational person.
`objectClass: organizationalPerson`	Specifies the `organizationalPerson` object class. This object class specification should be included because some LDAP clients require the existence of object class `organizationalPerson` during search operations for an organizational person.

The following is an example organizational person entry in LDIF format:

```
dn: cn=John Smith, ou=people, o=ibm.com
objectclass: top
objectclass: organizationalPerson
cn: John Smith
sn: Smith
givenname: John
uid: jsmith
ou: Marketing
ou: people
telephonenumber: 838-6004
```

2.4.2.4 LDIF File Example

Below is a simple LDIF file which contains an organizational unit *people* beneath the organization *ibm.com*. The entry of John Smith is the only data entry for people. Further on, there is an organizational unit called *marketing*. Note that John Smith is a member of the marketing department due to the attribute value pair `ou: marketing`.

```
dn: o=ibm.com
objectclass: top
```

```
objectclass: organization
o: ibm.com

dn: ou=People, o=ibm.com
objectclass: organizationalUnit
ou: people

dn: ou=marketing, o=ibm.com
objectclass: organisationalunit
ou: marketing

dn: cn=John Smith, ou=people, o=ibm.com
objectclass: top
objectclass: organizationalPerson
cn: John Smith
sn: Smith
givenname: John
uid: jsmith
ou: marketing
ou: people
telephonenumber: 838-6004
```

2.5 Platform Support

The architecture of LDAP does not depend on any operating system or hardware platform. LDAP was designed to run on multiple platforms, even with limited resources. The prerequisite is an operable TCP/IP communication stack.

LDAP client toolkits and server implementations are available for all major operating system platforms, and client functionality is contained in some applications already. Recent versions of Web browsers on various platforms, such as Netscape's Communicator or Microsoft's Internet Explorer, are already capable of searching LDAP directories, as shown in 1.6, "The Quick Start: A Public LDAP Example" on page 16.

Appendix B, "LDAP Products and Services" on page 143, gives you an overview of some products available on the market that are either LDAP servers, client packages or other products incorporating LDAP services.

Chapter 3. Designing and Maintaining an LDAP Directory

The two first chapters introduced LDAP, its basic concepts and principles. Although LDAP strictly refers to a protocol, we used this term in a broader context when describing LDAP servers or when outlining the contents of an LDAP directory. Introducing LDAP in an organization involves more than just adding another protocol. It requires thorough planning on how the directory contents should be designed and how it should be deployed in the physical infrastructure.

While discussing low-level details of designing a directory implementation, such as detailed performance tuning aspects or product selection criteria which are beyond the scope of this book, this chapter gives you an introductory understanding of what has to be considered when LDAP is to be introduced in an organization.

The first sections in this chapter describe some guidelines on how the design and implementation of the directory tree structure should be done. Then, implementing such a directory in a physical infrastructure having scalability, availability and manageability in mind is described, followed by some security and maintenance aspects of an LDAP directory deployment.

The last part of this chapter describes two hypothetical examples of LDAP implementations in a small and a large organization.

What is a Typical Directory?

The discussions that follow in this chapter often refer to typical White Pages directory implementations and the examples present common people directories. This approach was chosen for the sake of simplicity.

Please bear in mind, LDAP is *not* only suitable for people directories. An LDAP directory can hold almost any kind of information and can therefore be used for a much broader range of applications. The DEN initiative (see 5.4, "The Directory-Enabled Networks Initiative" on page 138) is just one example where an LDAP directory is being used for storing network configuration and topology data.

3.1 Directory Design Guidelines

Creating a design that has the flexibility to accommodate changes within the organization is probably the single most important task in implementing a directory service. This will help save time and money as the directory service grows. When designing the directory service, the project can be divided into several smaller projects: surveying the directory service contents, creating access control strategies, replication and partitioning strategies, and network planning (physical planning):

- Planning the directory content includes deciding on what data to store in the directory and how it will be arranged in the tree structure. When deciding on what to put into the directory, all the owners of data relevant to the contents of the directory tree in the organization should be identified. It is very probable that the information you will be choosing to put in the LDAP directory already resides on some other system in your organization. For example, the personnel department most likely already has databases with personnel information. Also be sure to make adequate use of processes already in place to administer that data even in the planned directory service.

- Data management and access control are both important when maintaining a directory service. Plans must be made to identify resources for keeping the data up to date and identifying resources with the authority to decide on access control policies regarding the data residing in the directory tree.

- In sizing the directory service, consideration must be taken to which clients will be accessing what data, from where, and how often. If there are client applications which use the directory extensively, consideration must be taken to ensure that the network availability and bandwidth are sufficient between the application servers and the directory servers. If there are network bottlenecks, they must be identified because there may be needs to replicate data into remote LANs.

3.1.1 Defining the Data Model

There are many steps involved in designing a directory tree, such as deciding on the kind of data that the entries will contain, what schema to use and finally how the entries are going to be arranged in the tree structure. During design, several different aspects must be taken into account:

- What type of application/applications will use the directory?

- Will the LDAP service be participating with an X.500 directory service?

- How will the organizations infrastructure be mapped into the directory?

- What are the requirements for manageability and scalability?

3.1.1.1 Directory Data

Planning the directory's data is the most important aspect of the directory planning activities, and it is probably the most time-consuming aspect as well.

A considerable amount of the time spent planning the directory data will most likely be spent surveying the organization to locate all the data stores where directory information is managed. As this survey is performed, expect to find that some kinds of data are not well managed; some processes may be inefficient, inadequate, or nonexistent altogether; and some kinds of data may not be available at all. All of these issues should be addressed before finishing a data-planning phase.

We start by looking at the requirements on the data to be used in the directory service. Some types of data are better suited for a directory service than others. Ideal candidates in a directory service have some of the following characteristics:

As already discussed in Chapter 1, a directory service is not a file system, a file server, an FTP server, a Web server, or a relational database. Therefore, large, unstructured objects of data should not be put in the directory. For that kind of data, a server more appropriate for the task should be used. However, it is appropriate to store pointers to these kinds of applications within the directory service through the use of FTP, HTTP, or other types of accesses.

The data should typically be read much more often than it is written. This is because directory services usually are tuned for read operations; write operations are more expensive in terms of resource utilization than reads, and they may impact the directory server's performance in typical directory server implementations.

Another "rule of thumb" is that the data should typically be accessed from more than just one system or client. For example, an employee's preference settings for a specific application may not be meaningful to put in the directory if that application is only run on the employee's single workstation. If the user wants to run this application on different systems, such as a mail client application, then the application would certainly benefit from a central directory for storing user preferences. This would allow the employee to use the same setup on multiple systems or even platforms within the organization.

Having in mind the types of data suitable and unsuitable for use in a directory, it is now possible to survey what the directory service data will be. In doing this, it may be helpful to do the following:

• Determine what directory-enabled applications to deploy and what their data needs are.

- Survey the organization and identify where the data comes from (such as Windows NT or Novell NetWare directories, Human Resources databases, e-mail systems, and so forth.).

- Determine who needs access to the data, particularly the organization's mission-critical applications. Find out if those applications can directly access and/or update the directory.

- For each piece of data, determine the location where it will be mastered, who owns the data—that is, who is responsible for ensuring that the data is up-to-date.

- For each piece of data, determine the name of the attribute(s) that you will use to represent the data in the directory and the object class(es) (the type of entry) that the data will be stored on.

- If data is going to be imported from other sources, develop a strategy for both bulk imports and incremental updates. Try to limit the number of applications that can change the data. Doing this will help ensure the data integrity while reducing the organization's administration.

- Identify duplications and data that is not actually used or required. Harmonize the data by eliminating such duplications and discard unnecessary data.

Having decided on the type of data to use in the directory service, what the directory will be used for and how the data will be updated, it is possible to start structuring the data. Structuring data is done by designing a *schema*, choosing a *directory suffix*, *branching* the directory tree and finally creating a *naming style* for the directory entries. We explain these activities in the sections that follow.

3.1.1.2 Directory Schema

A schema is the collection of attribute type definitions and object class definitions. A server uses these to determine how to match a filter or attribute against the attributes of a specific entry and whether to permit given attribute(s) to be added. See also 2.2.1, "The Information Model" on page 25, for more details.

When deciding on the design of the schema, there are a few things to consider. The LDAP specifications include a standard schema for a typical white pages directory (RFC 2256, *A Summary of the X.500(96) User Schema for use with LDAPv3*). Vendors ship schemas with their LDAP server products that may include some extensions to support special features they feel are common and useful to their client applications. Work at the IETF is in progress to create standard schemas for a broad range of applications.

Regardless of the type of information contained in the directory server, the standard schema, some of which is based on the X.500 standard, should not be modified. If this standard schema proves to be too limiting for the intended use, it can be extended to support the unique requirements. Standard schema elements, however, should not be deleted. Doing so can lead to interoperability problems between different directory services and LDAP clients.

It is important to use a consistent schema within the directory server because LDAP-enabled application clients locate entries in the directory by searching for object classes or attributes and their associated values. If the schemes are inconsistent, then it becomes virtually impossible to locate information in the directory tree efficiently. An example of an inconsistent schema is a situation where an attribute is used to store a specific kind of information, and then later a different attribute is used to store the exact same kind of data, for example when both attributes, telephoneNumber and phone contained the same data.

Most LDAP-enabled application clients are designed to work with a specific, well-defined schema. Shrink-wrapped standard applications most likely only work with a standard schema. This is an important reason why LDAP-based directory services should support at least the standard LDAP schema. Then, the schema may be extended as the site discovers site-specific needs that are not met by the standard schema.

Private Schema?

The previous section points out that the use of a standard schema is beneficial and that specific changes can be done as long as they are additions.

You may, however, create your own, private schema. But when doing so, you must take into consideration that compatibility to any other LDAP service may be lost and that your application clients have to be aware of that private schema.

3.1.1.3 Choosing a Suffix

When deciding on suffixes, where a suffix is the root DN of a directory tree as described in 2.2.2.2, "Suffixes and Referrals" on page 32, it is basically a good idea to use the same naming structure for LDAP as it is used for X.500. Using the X.500 methodology would lead to choosing a suffixes like:

o=ibm, c=us or ou=austin, o=ibm

This method will set the root of the directory tree to a specific organization in a specific country or to a specific organization and organizational unit. However, it is not necessary to do this, unless there are plans to participate in an X.500 directory service, since LDAP does not require any specific format for the DN naming convention. In LDAP, the directory suffix can be chosen freely to reflect the organizations distinct name. Another method that you can use, if the X.500 does not seem appropriate, is to use the DNS naming model when choosing the directory suffix. This would result in a suffix using the `domainComponent` attribute, for example: `dc=xyz.se`, `dc=abc.us`, or `dc=abc.com`.

The design of the directory schema and definition of the suffix makes it possible to start populating the tree. But, before doing so, the naming structure must be put in place. We have divided the discussion on naming structure creation into the two sections that follow: (1) Branching of the directory tree and (2) naming style for the entries.

3.1.1.4 Branching the Directory Tree

Choosing to branch a directory tree based on the organizational structure, such as departments (see Figure 16), can lead to a large administrative overhead if the organization is very dynamic and changes often. On the other hand, branching the tree based on geography may restrict the ability to reflect information about the organizational structure. A branching methodology that is flexible, and which still reflects enough information about the organization, must be created.

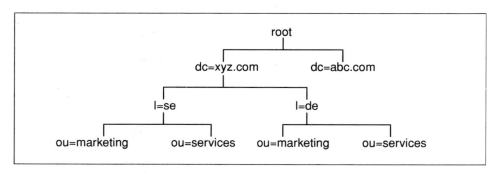

Figure 16. DNS-Type Naming Model for the Directory Tree

Because the structure of organizations often changes considerably over time, the aim should be to branch the tree in such a way as to minimize the number of necessary changes to the directory tree once the organization has changed. Note that renaming a department entry, for example, has the effect of requiring a change of the DNs of all entries below its branch point. This has an undesirable impact on the service for several reasons. Alias entries and certain attributes or ordinary entries, such as seeAlso and secretary, use DNs to maintain links with other entries. These references are one-way only, and LDAP currently offers no support to automatically update all references to an entry once its DN changes. The impact of renaming branches is illustrated in the following example.

When adding employees to their respective departments, it would be possible to create distinguished names (DN) like cn=John Smith, ou=Marketing, l=se, dc=xyz.com. If John Smith should at a later time move to another department, his DN will have to change. This results in changing all entries regarding access rights and more. If John Smith's DN had been set to cn=John Smith, ou=employees, l=se, dc=xyz.com, then this would not be a problem, as depicted in see Figure 17. An attribute describing which department he belongs to (ou=marketing) could be added to his entry to include this information.

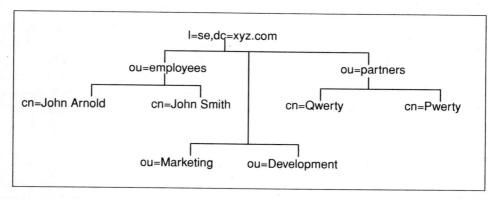

Figure 17. Modified Tree Representation of an Organization

Other criteria that may or should be considered when branching the directory tree include:

- Physical separation and/or separate management responsibilities

    If your organization has separate units that are either physically separated or have their own management authorities, you might have a "natural" requirement to split and separate parts of the DIT.

- Human or machine clients

    A general "rule of thumb" says that the DIT should be reasonably shallow unless there are strong reasons to design deep branching levels down the directory tree. If the directory information is primarily searched and read by human users—that is, if users manually type in search criteria—the DIT should provide the information in an intuitive manner so that finding information is not limited to system specialists. If, on the other hand, the information is primarily retrieved from programs, other rules more suitable for that application can be followed.

- Performance and system characteristics

  Although it should not be the primary design goal to analyze and meet the strengths and circumvent weaknesses of a specific server (as they may change with new software releases or other vendor products), it is good practice to have some characteristics of the implementation in mind when branching a DIT.

3.1.1.5 Naming Style

The first goal of naming is to provide unique identifiers for entries. Once this is achieved, the next major goal in naming entries should be to make querying of the directory tree intuitive. Support for a naming structure which enables the use of *user friendly naming* is desirable (see the discussion on multicomponent RDNs below). Other considerations, such as accurately reflecting the organizational structure of an organization, should be disregarded if it has a negative effect of creating complex DNs, thus making normal querying nonintuitive. If we take a look at the X.500 view on naming, we see that the X.501 standard specifies that *"RDNs are intended to be long-lived so that the users of the Directory can store the distinguished names of objects..."*, and *"It is preferable that distinguished names of objects which humans have to deal with be user-friendly."* (excerpt from *The Directory – Overview of Concepts, Models and Services*, CCITT 1988, cited in RFC 1617).

Multicomponent relative distinguished names can be created by using more than one component selected from the set of the attributes of the entry to be named. This is useful when there are, for example, two persons named *John Smith* in one department. The use of multicomponent relative distinguished names allows one to avoid artificial naming values such as cn=John Smith 1 or cn=John Smith 2. Attributes which could be used as the additional naming attribute include: Title, room number, telephone number, and user ID, resulting in a RDN like title=Dr, cn=John Smith, creating a more user friendly naming model.

A consistent approach to naming people is especially important when the directory stores information about people. Client applications will also be better able to assist users if entries have names conforming to a common format, or at least to a very limited set of formats. It is practical if the RDN follows such a format.

In general, the standard attribute types should be used as documented in the standards whenever possible. It is important to decide, within the organization, which attributes to use for what purpose and not to deviate from that structure, as mentioned earlier in 3.1.1.1, "Directory Data" on page 59.

It is also important that the choice of a naming strategy not be made on the basis of the possibilities of the currently available client applications. For example, it is questionable to use commonName of the form "surname firstname" merely because a client application presents results in a more satisfactory order by so doing. Use the best structure for people's names, and adapt or design the client applications accordingly.

We have discussed some aspects of directory design. After all, it needs to be pointed out that there is no single correct way to design a directory. To be able to build a more objective picture of the naming methodology, we recommend that several sources of information are compared. Often, vendors will have their own implementation guides that reflect different angles of views for this aspect. See also A.4, "Other Sources" on page 140, for information on literature in this area.

3.1.2 Security Policy

Having designed the directory tree, we now need to decide on a security policy. A security policy should be strong enough to prevent sensitive information from being modified or retrieved by unauthorized users while simple enough that administration is kept simple so authorized parties can easily access it. Ease of administration is very important when it comes to designing a security policy. A too complex security policy can lead to mistakes that either prevent people from accessing information that they should have access to, or allow people to modify or retrieve directory information that they should not have access to.

The security policy that needs to be designed for the directory service is a reflection of the:

- Kind of information that will be stored in the directory
- Ways in which clients will be accessing the directory
- Ways which will be used to update and manage the directory
- Acceptable administration effort for security

To reach these goals, two basic areas must be considered and the following question must be answered: What level of security is needed when clients identify themselves to the directory server, and what methodology will be used when authorizing access to the different kinds of information in the directory?

3.1.2.1 Authentication
Conceptually, directory authentication can be thought of as logging in to the directory. LDAP terminology, however, usually refers to this operation as binding to the directory.

Generally, bind operations consist of providing the equivalent of a user ID and a password. However, in the case of an LDAP directory, the user ID is actually a distinguished name (or a distinguished name derived from a user ID). The distinguished name used to access the directory is referred to as the bind DN.

So, what level of authentication should be considered? There are, generally speaking, three different approaches:

No Authentication
This is the simplest approach, which might be perfectly suitable for most directories when all users are equally granted read (or even write) access to all data. There is no need for user authentication when this is the case.

Basic Authentication
This lets the client bind by entering a DN and a password. Using basic authentication will not ensure integrity and confidentiality of the login data since it is being sent over the network in a readable form (see also 2.3.2, "Basic Authentication" on page 44).

Secure Authentication
SASL (Simple Authentication and Security Layer) is an extensible authentication framework. It was added to LDAP Version 3, and it supports Kerberos and other security methods, like S/Key. SASL provides the possibility to securely authenticate LDAP clients and LDAP directory servers. There is a so called EXTERNAL mechanism in SASL that allows the use of authentication identity information from security layers external to the SASL layer. One possibility is to use the authentication information from SSL. SSL is generally used to secure the connection between a client and a server through the exchange of certificates. The client certificate can get used through SASL as authentication identity.

SASL is already used within several Internet protocols including IMAP4 and POP3 (mail server protocols) and is described in more details in 2.3.3, "Simple Authentication and Security Layer (SASL)" on page 45.

It is possible that there is a need for both basic and secure authentication. The choice will be dependent on the security policies in the organization's networks and what type of access rights the different types clients will have when communicating with the server. For example, when setting up server-to-server communication, it may be valuable to use strong, secure authentication since server-to-server communication will often rely on unrestricted access to each other's tree structures, including individual entries access settings. On the other hand, for client-to-server communication, where clients only have read access to names, phone numbers, and mail addresses, there is most likely no need for anything but basic authentication.

When using secure authentication, it is possible to choose from different methods depending on the vendors' implementations, for example Kerberos or SSL. If Kerberos is not already deployed in the organization's intranet, then it will probably be sensible to use SSL, since support for SSL is included in most popular LDAP clients. When using SSL, it is possible for the server to authenticate to the client by using its server certificate. A server certificate can be thought of as a secure, digital signature that unequivocally identifies a server. It has been generated and registered with a trusted certifying authority, also known as a Certificate Authority (CA), such as the United States Postal Service CA or the IBM World Registry CA. Also, when using server certificates, an encrypted communication can be established between the client and server, enabling a secure basic authentication of the client to the server. Please refer to 2.3.3.1, "SSL and TLS" on page 47, for more information on certificates and SSL.

Using SSL server certificates will be particularly interesting when setting up LDAP services on insecure networks, such as the Internet/extranet. This will enable the clients to verify the identity of the server and to encrypt communication of the basic authentication from the clients to the server on the insecure networks.

When using basic authentication, administration of passwords on the directory server will be necessary and may impose some administration overhead. If SSL client certificates are used, then an appropriate infrastructure will be needed to support the certificate generation and administration. This is usually done by separate certificate servers. Client certificate deployment is beyond the scope of this book, but it ought to be mentioned that LDAP supports storing client public keys and certificates in the entries.

3.1.2.2 Authorization

The data in the directory tree will have to be protected in different ways. Certain information must be searchable for everybody, some must be readable, and most of it will be write protected. In LDAP Version 3, there are no defined attributes to handle this. As a result, vendors support their own implementations of authorization. This is done by different implementations of access control lists (ACLs).

ACLs are used to define access rules to the different entries in the directory tree. As an example of an ACL implementation, Figure 18 shows the IBM eNetwork LDAP directory server's implementation of ACL attribute entries. The pertinent control attributes used here are: `aclsource`, `aclpropagate`, and `aclentry`, where the latter, for example, is the attribute that specifies who has access to the entry and what level of access he or she has. In the example shown in Figure 18, `cn=John Arnold, ou=Austin, o=xyz, c=us` has read, write, search and compare (rwsc) rights for normal, sensitive and critical data (the entry is highlighted and spilled into three lines in the example below).

```
dn: ou=Austin, o=xyz, c=US
objectclass: top
objectclass: organizationalUnit
ou: Austin
description: Austin Office
entryowner: access-id:cn=admin,o=xyz,c=US
inheritoncreate: TRUE
ownerpropagate: TRUE
aclpropagate: TRUE
ownersource: default
aclsource: OU=AUSTIN,O=xyz,C=US
aclentry: access-id:CN=John
Arnold,OU=Austin,O=xyz,C=us:object:a:normal:rwsc:
sensitive:rwsc:critical:rwsc
aclentry: group:CN=ANYBODY:normal:rsc
```

Figure 18. Sample ACL Attribute Entry

When setting up access control lists, it is important to do it with the goal to minimize the administration later on. It is good to try and delegate the access control hierarchically.

An example of this could be the following: An individual, say John Arnold, needs to protect sensitive information. Two groups have been created for this purpose, owned by John Arnold (see Table 14). Entries can be added and deleted by John Arnold to his "own" groups without intervention of the directory service administrators.

Table 14. ACL Structure for Web Content Administration Using Two Groups

Group Name	Owner	Group Members
cn=editor	cn=John Arnold	cn=user1
cn=readers	cn=John Arnold	cn=user2 ou=marketing

According to Table 14, John Arnold has added user1 to the editor group and user2 and the group called marketing to the readers group, thus enabling user1 to edit the contents, and enabling user2 and the people in the marketing group to read the contents.

3.1.3 Physical Design

Physical design involves building a network and server infrastructures to support availability, scalability and manageability. Methods to do this in LDAP are partitioning and replication (replication is actually not standardized in LDAP Version 3, but most vendors do have an implementation). In this section, we concentrate on deployment issues regarding when partitioning and/or replication is appropriate when trying to reach the goals of availability, scalability and manageability, and what the trade-offs are.

3.1.3.1 Availability

Availability for a directory service may not be an issue in cases where the directory is not business-critical. However, if the use of the service becomes mission-critical, the need to design a highly available system is required. Designing a highly available system involves more than what is supported in LDAP. The components from LDAP that are needed are partitioning and replication. Since high availability involves eliminating single points of failure or reducing their impact, it is necessary to have redundant hardware, software and networks to spread the risk.

A simple approach to create a highly available directory service is to create a master and a slave directory server, each one on its own physical machine. By replicating the data, we have eliminated the single point of failure for both hardware and software failures. This solution with a master and one or more slave servers normally provides for high availability for read functions to the LDAP servers. Write requests can only be directed to the master server. If high availability is required for write access, additional effort is necessary. Neither read-only nor read/write replication is supported natively by the LDAP standards, but vendors may have implemented their own mechanisms. Replication solutions can also be constructed using the export/import facilities of LDAP servers or with additional, custom-designed software tools.

A mechanism must be added to handle client redirection if one server fails. This can be done manually or semi-automatically by a DNS switchover, or automatically with a load-balancing technique by using a router designed for this, as shown in Figure 19. Such a router forwards client requests to one of the servers based on configurable criteria. It is important that the router supports stateful protocols; that is, subsequent requests from the same client need to be forwarded to the same server. There are several products on the market from different vendors to do this, such as IBM's eNetwork Dispatcher (see `www.ics.raleigh.ibm.com/netdispatch/`) or Cisco Systems' Local Director (`www.cisco.com`).

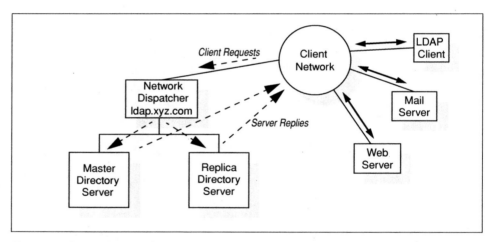

Figure 19. Setup of a Load Balancing, Replicated LDAP Cluster

There is also the issue of network bandwidth and its reliability to take into consideration. In some cases, it may be necessary to distribute a replica into another LAN with slow network connections to the master, as shown in Figure 20. This can also be done with any means of replicating an LDAP server (remember that replication is not included in the LDAP standards, thus you have to use vendor product support or your own methods). The primary server for a particular client may be the directory server on the client's own LAN, and the secondary will then be the central master server, accessed over the WAN.

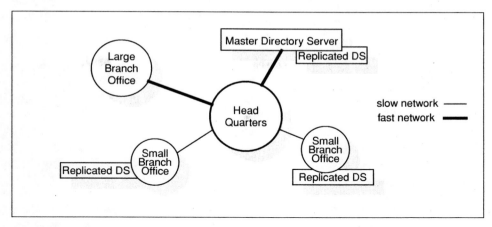

Figure 20. Example of an Organization's Network

If the method of spreading the risk is used to create high availability, it is possible to partition the directory tree and to distribute it to different locations, LANs, or departments, as shown as an example in Figure 21. As a side-effect, depending on how the directory tree is branched and distributed to these servers, each location, department or LAN administrator could then easily manage their own part of the directory tree on a local machine, if this is a requirement. If a single server failed in such a configuration, then only a portion of the whole directory would be affected.

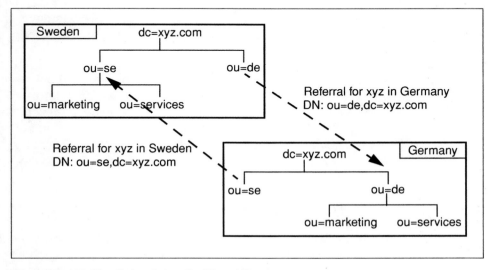

Figure 21. Handling Referrals in a Partitioned Namespace

A combination of the two methods explained above could be used to create a dynamic, distributed, highly available directory service.

3.1.3.2 Scalability

As more and more applications use and rely on a directory service, the need to scale the directory for high load tolerance increases. Scaling up directory servers is done much the same way, either by increasing availability or by upgrading hardware performance. As is the case when increasing availability, we have to rely on functions outside the LDAP standard as well as LDAP replication and partitioning. The round-robin DNS or the load-balancing router are good tools to scale an LDAP server site, as explained in the previous section 3.1.3.1, "Availability" on page 69.

Scalability may be affected by network performance, therefore requiring local directory servers in LANs.

3.1.3.3 Manageability

Management of an LDAP service, as far as contents management for the directory contents is concerned, has been elaborated in 2.4, "Manageability" on page 49. A product that supports LDAP contents management will also be discussed in B.3, "Tivoli User Administration: LDAP Endpoint" on page 147. This section concentrates on manageability issues specific to the design phase of an LDAP service.

Manageability aspects involve almost all parts of a directory design. Here is where trade-offs may have to be made regarding scalability, availability, flexibility, and manageability. The level of scalability and availability are both related to cost in hardware and software and, as a drag-along, cost of overall systems management.

One important question to ask in a directory design about manageability is whether and how all information providers are able to furnish reliable, correct and consistent directory data to the LDAP service. If this cannot be assured, there will be a chance for errors and inconsistencies in the LDAP directory data. If such problems are considered critical for the clients using the LDAP service, tools must be provided that can detect and maybe even correct these errors.

To create a high availability environment, it is necessary to replicate and/or partition the directory, as discussed in the previous sections. Although not directly related to LDAP, it should be mentioned that adequate systems management tools and skills must be available to run such a fairly complex environment. In addition, one of the manageability concerns regarding replication might be the need to ensure an ample level of consistency. A master LDAP server might have been updated with new information while a replica server still runs with the old, outdated information. The required level of consistency is largely dependent on the needs of the client applications using the service. If there is a requirement for currency and consistency among replicated servers, additional means must be provided to ensure this.

Replication will also affect backup and disaster/recovery procedures. Processes will be needed to handle recovery of master servers and how synchronization of slaves will be handled. Since replication is outside the current standard for LDAP, it is necessary to study the vendors' implementation in order to find adequate solutions.

Partitioning the directory enables local servers to own their own data, depending on schema and branching design. This increases flexibility when maintaining data, but increases the complexity of referral handling. A clear method of linking the name space together will have to be formulated to ensure consistent referrals in the directory service name space such that the logical name space is still a whole. Also, each local server may have to be administered and maintained locally, requiring staff with operating system and LDAP knowledge.

3.2 Migration Planning

Having done all the planning and design work to introduce LDAP as a new directory service, one more important task has to follow. Remember that the job of designing an LDAP directory very likely started with an analysis of currently available data and the various locations and services where directory data might be stored and serviced from. For example, there might be several LAN-based directories installed and operational already in your organization, such as IBM Warp Server domains, Microsoft Windows NT/95 domains, Novell NetWare domains, or other databases with directory-type information.

In most cases, introducing LDAP will not be an introduction of a new service from scratch, but some kind of a migration from existing services to LDAP. Once your organization has decided to move to an open, vendor-independent directory service, which describes LDAP perfectly, you have to carefully analyze if and how current directories can participate in, benefit from, or even be migrated to an LDAP directory infrastructure.

Bear in mind that such a migration is not just a software or application replacement; it is also a chance and the right time to redesign and harmonize the data in your directories (Figure 22).

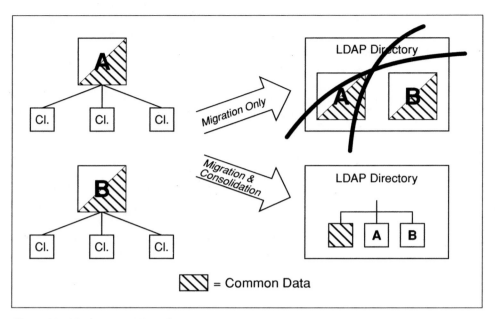

Figure 22. Migration and Data Consolidation

Because migrating current directory services to LDAP may not be a trivial or risk-free undertaking, your decision might be to run and maintain proprietary directory services in parallel with LDAP for some period of time (while this is certainly not textbook advice, it may be considered for practical reasons). This might also be necessary when you need to keep some of the proprietary services running for some time that cannot be supported with LDAP. Another common reason for running LDAP and other directory services in parallel might be a shortage in skills or staff personnel.

Figure 23 graphically shows a possible migration scenario as it might be planned over time. This low-risk approach, however, involves some additional maintenance effort since there are parallel directories to maintain for a certain amount of time. The basic idea behind the scenario depicted in Figure 23 is:

1. Start building up an LDAP directory service infrastructure that is properly designed to accommodate the needs.

2. Populate the LDAP directory with the data for the first service to be migrated. Keep the LDAP directory data in sync with the original data.

3. Migrate the clients to the new LDAP service.

4. After successful migration, the original service can be sunset.

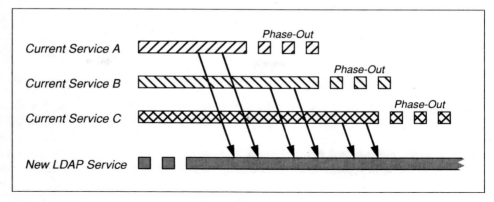

Figure 23. Migration from Existing Directory Services to LDAP

While this approach sounds reasonably simple in theory, there might be some complications in the real world. A major obstruction might be proprietary add-on services in the current vendor-specific directories that are beyond the capabilities of LDAP. (For this reason, you might consider it an important pre-planning step to not use proprietary functions whatsoever in vendor-specific directory services to ensure a smooth migration to open standards.) If planning for a migration, it should also be considered that, according to their public program announcements, vendor-specific directory services, such as Novell's NDS or Microsoft's Active Directory, support an LDAP interface. Using this interface, LDAP clients can access data in these directories.

Running parallel directory services also means that the LDAP directory must be kept in sync with the current directories (depending on your requirements for data currency and consistency). This can be achieved in different ways. Depending on the decision on when the primary data administration is going to be moved to LDAP, data may still be administered in the "old" directory while clients already use the new LDAP service. In this case, the LDIF file format (see 2.4.2, "LDAP Data Interchange Format (LDIF)" on page 50), along with the supporting import/export facilities, might be an easy method for keeping directories synchronized.

The migration approach just described involves little risks because there always is a backout method in case a migration step fails. Clients may be migrated within a time period, which is especially useful in large installations. New services may experience a delay when problems are encountered after their introduction. Migration of a complete service at one time imposes a much higher risk because both servers and clients (including applications) have to ready immediately. The only (usual) backout solution is to go back and (re)install the old environment. The decision on which scenario to follow largely depends on the size of the installation, the risk that can be taken, and the possibilities to run directory services in parallel.

3.3 Example Scenarios

Earlier in this chapter, we discussed design, deployment, security, and maintenance of a directory service. In this section, we summarize in two examples the specific considerations that need to be taken when an LDAP implementation is being designed. The first example looks at a hypothetical, small organization, like a small company or a department within a larger organization. The second example scenario describes an implementation in a large organization.

3.3.1 Small Organization

The scenario in this example assumes an organization of a few hundred employees that has no plans of future integration with X.500. The organization can be a small company or an isolated department within an enterprise. The LDAP directory service to be implemented, as described in the following subsections, can be described as a minimum implementation without any sophisticated exploitation.

3.3.1.1 Directory Data

The directory service will initially be used by a white pages application, a Web server and a mailserver application. The data to be put in the database will be taken from the personnel database and combined with records from an IT database that contains e-mail addresses. The intention is to add and remove employee entries automatically to or from the LDAP directory after the database in the personnel department has been changed. This will be done with a C program using the LDAP-API to interact with the LDAP directory. Since data consistency is not crucial, this program will be run as a batch job only once per day, presumably at night. As an option, the C program could be smart enough to detect changes in the personnel database and propagate those changes to the LDAP directory. Alternatively, the program could just extract all employee information from the personnel database and re-create all entries in the LDAP directory. The latter, simpler approach has the advantage of ensuring consistency within the LDAP directory (with a maximum of one day delay), but has the disadvantage of a short service interruption when the whole directory is purged and reloaded.

3.3.1.2 Directory Schema

The object classes to be used for the employee entries include:

```
top
person
organizationalPerson
inetOrgPerson
mailRecipient
```

These will cover the needs for white pages and e-mail application.

3.3.1.3 Directory Suffix, Branching and Naming

The directory suffix for the company is set to its internet domain, `dc=xyz.com` since there will be no integration with X.500.

The organization consists of three departments: Marketing, Services, and Accounting.

The employee and group entries will be placed directly under the root entry, `dc=xyz.com`. This creates a flexible, flat organization, which works fine for an organization with only a relatively small number of entries, say a few hundred.

The RDN of the employees will be the `commonName` attribute, and for those with the same `commonName` an `organizationalUnit` attribute will be added to the RDN. For example, John Smith in Marketing will have the entry:

```
dn: ou=Marketing cn=John Smith, dc=xyz.com
objectclass: top
objectclass: person
objectclass: organizationalPerson
objectclass: inetOrgPerson
cn: John Smith
sn: Smith
givenname: John
uid: jsmith
ou: Marketing
employeenumber: 091377
telephonenumber: 838-6004
```

and the other person named John Smith in Accounting:

```
dn: ou=Accounting cn=John Smith, dc=xyz.com
objectclass: top
objectclass: person
objectclass: organizationalPerson
objectclass: inetOrgPerson
cn: John Smith
sn: Smith
givenname: John
uid: josmith
```

```
ou: Accounting
employeenumber: 235532
telephonenumber: 838-5501
```

An excerpt of the directory tree containing four sample entries can be seen in Figure 24.

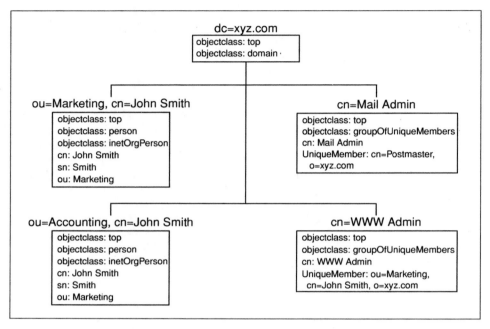

Figure 24. Example Directory Tree with Attributes for a Small Organization

3.3.1.4 Security

There is no need for anything but basic authentication since the company runs an isolated intranet behind a firewall that is considered secure. The only requirement is that the users' entries contain the attributes `uid` and `userPassword` for the LDAP server to verify the users' identities. Access control is set up such that all users can read, but only administrators can write to the directory.

3.3.1.5 Physical Design

In this small organization, there is no need for multiple, redundant directory servers because the directory service is not considered mission-critical for the following two reasons:

- The data in the LDAP server can be re-created in case it is lost.

- A service interruption of a few hours after a hardware or software failure is considered acceptable.

Therefore, a single machine will be used as the LDAP server, which may even be used for other purposes, such as mail server. However, a backup/restore procedure needs to be put in place that allows the administrator to restore (reinstall) the machine in an acceptable amount of time.

3.3.1.6 Maintenance

Maintenance in the described installation must at least cover basic systems management and monitoring. This includes monitoring (and alerting in case of a problem) of system resources and processes to ensure a reliable operation of the LDAP service. If the simple approach was chosen to purge and reload the LDAP directory on a regular basis, then chances are inherently small that an inconsistency would exist in the directory unless the purge/reload process failed (which, of course, should be carefully monitored) or the source database was inconsistent. If only updates are carried on to the LDAP server and/or local changes are done in the directory, there might be a need for a tool that checks validity and consistency of the directory. Local changes might be necessary to resolve password problems or if a scheduled update is too late for some reason.

3.3.2 Large Organization

This second example assumes an organization with thousands of employees and plans for later integrating with X.500. The organization is a multinational enterprise called ABC.

3.3.2.1 Directory Data

ABC is a company consisting of numerous departments, many being the size of a small organization like the one described in the last example (see 3.3.1, "Small Organization" on page 76). The LDAP service will be used for white pages and for an e-mail application. There will also be a Web service using custom client profiles to create personal Web pages. LDAP will also contain client certificates to enable secure mail and SSL authentication towards the intranet servers.

The Human Resources (HR) department will be in charge of updating the directory regarding employee information, except for e-mail addresses, certificates and client passwords, which will be handled by the IT security department. They will all create and furnish LDIF files for the bulk imports into the directory when the service is initiated. After that, they will be using a customized C program to keep the LDAP directory in sync with their department's databases. Alternatively, update LDIF files could be created that are then subsequently imported into the LDAP directory, either on a scheduled basis or on request (for example, whenever such an LDIF has been created as a result of a change).

The requirements on scalability and manageability are high; 7x24 is required for availability.

3.3.2.2 Directory Schema

It has been decided that the standard X.500 schema be used for compatibility reasons since there may be requirements on participating in a public X.500 service. The object classes from which the employee entries are created will contain:

```
top
person
organizationalPerson
inetOrgPerson
mailRecipient
```

The object class `certificationAuthority` will be added to the organization's Certifying Authority entry.

3.3.2.3 Directory Suffix, Branching and Naming

There will be several suffixes needed. One is required for the central office server (ldap.abc.us), located in New York, being set to o=abc, c=us. This will be the organization's root LDAP server, which refers to all underlying servers. Figure 25 shows the setup for the two regional offices in Sweden and Germany. These regional offices will have different suffixes: ou=Stockholm, o=abc, c=se and ou=Mainz, o=abc, c=de. The LDAP server in Stockholm, Sweden, has an additional suffix for performance reasons because it communicates very often (assumption) with the New York office and therefore has their directory tree replicated to Stockholm and placed under the suffix ou=New York, o=abc, c=us.

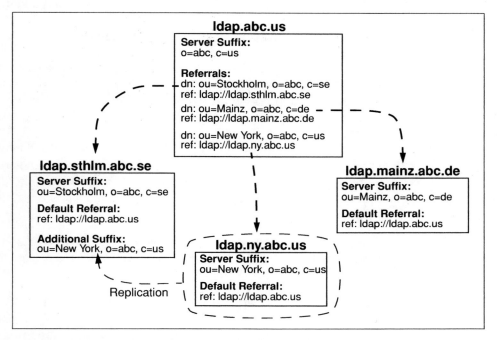

Figure 25. *Partitioned Namespace Setup for the ABC Organization*

The employees' entries are placed directly under their countries office DN, creating DNs like cn=Erik Eriksson, ou=Stockholm, o=abc, c=se. In cases where duplicate names are encountered the attribute mail is added to the RDN.

You might have noticed the notation ldap://<server> in Figure 25. These are LDAP URLs (uniform resource locators), very similar to the well known HTML URLs (http://<server>/...). More information about LDAP URLs can be found in 4.4, "LDAP URLs" on page 120.

3.3.2.4 Security

Security on the world wide network of the organization is not considered completely safe due to its overall size (increased risk of inside hackers) and the fact that parts of it are not under the organization's control. It is difficult to control who is connected to the network. Therefore, SSL will be used to secure communication between the directory servers themselves and between the application servers and directory servers (but not between clients and the directory servers). To enable SSL there needs to be a userCertificate attribute in the servers' DN entries. The clients will use basic authentication with no encryption of the network messages, thus only requiring the `uid` and `userPassword` attributes to be included in the employees' entries.

3.3.2.5 Physical Design

The offices in Stockholm and New York have a need for performance and high availability. Ample performance is needed because of the load from all the local clients and the e-mail and Web applications using the directory server. The high availability is necessary due to the critical nature of mail and the content on the Web where they keep their document system. Future applications may rely even more on the directory service. The directory service is therefore run on duplicated servers. A load-balancing router (for example the IBM eNetwork Dispatcher) shall be used to route directory requests to the least loaded machine, or if a machine is down, then all requests will exclusively routed to the other server.

Because of the organization's slow network connection between the offices in Europe and the US, the New York directory tree is replicated to the Stockholm directory server (see Figure 25).

The office in Mainz, Germany, is relatively small, and thus, they feel it is not necessary to have replicated servers because a failure does not create a critical business situation. Since the load will be small, one machine can serve as directory server without introducing any performance bottlenecks.

There is a separate server in place for the root directory of the organization only. It could be placed in the same physical machine(s) as the New York office directory service. Having a separate server (or actually two for redundancy) allows for rapid growth and also separates the relatively static root directory service from the more dynamic subtree service. The root server(s) can handle all requests at the corporate top level (ldap.abc.us) and will then refer these requests to the appropriate server(s). For example, requests for an entry in the Stockholm directory tree, made to the New York server (ldap.ny.abc.us), will refer to the root server (ldap.abc.us), which in turn will refer to the Stockholm server (ldap.sthlm.abc.se).

Figure 26 depicts the organization's global configuration as far as LDAP directory service is concerned. Please also refer to Figure 25 to better understand the proposed layout.

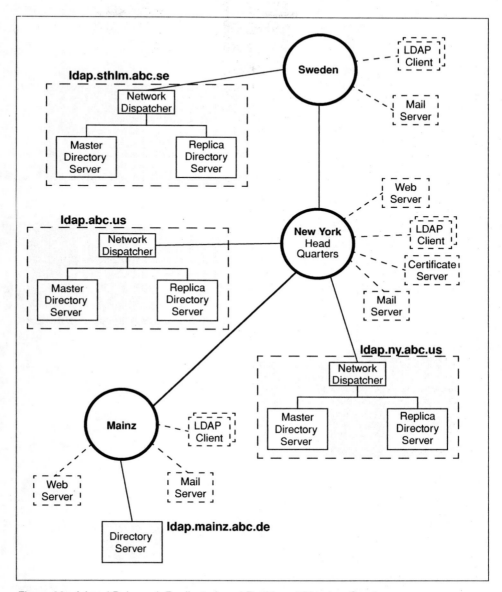

Figure 26. A Load Balanced, Replicated, and Partitioned Directory Service

3.3.2.6 Maintenance

As with all production systems, basic systems monitoring, including alerting in case of problems, is necessary for all involved systems to ensure a reliable operation. This includes surveillance of system resource utilizations, processes, and console messages.

There are automated procedures and processes involved that need to be monitored and, depending on the organization's operations guidelines, tested on a regular bases. They are:

- Propagation of changes of the data to the LDAP directory
- Master/replica replication
- Operation of the network dispatcher (load balancing and failure handling)
- Replication of the New York directory to the server in Sweden
- Basic system backup and restore

Having paired servers allows an administrator to schedule maintenance on single machines without interruption of the service. This might be necessary for the installation of software updates or hardware upgrades

There is very little maintenance overhead specific to LDAP, other than to ensure a reliable environment as stated above. Security-related issues, such as password updates or certificate management, might require some attention. Only when the LDAP data is manipulated directly on the LDAP server(s), thus introducing a new level of possible errors, some tools for checking consistency and validity of the data may be desirable.

Chapter 4. Building LDAP-Enabled Applications

The amount of directory-type information is growing very rapidly. This information is often distributed in proprietary databases implemented on different hardware and software platforms. LDAP is an ideal tool to manage this data because it is a powerful but easy-to-handle protocol which can be run by an LDAP-enabled client, for example a Web browser, on various platforms. It therefore offers an easy way to access this data.

The term *LDAP client* is used here in a very general way. In fact, it could be any type of application, for example a word processor that uses LDAP to check the receiver address of a letter.

This chapter introduces the LDAP Application Programming Interface (API) for the C language and Java to enable clients or more general applications to access information stored in LDAP enabled directories. It is based mainly on the appropriate RFCs or Internet Drafts, depending on which API, C language or Java, we refer to.

As far as the C language API is concerned, RFC 1823, *The LDAP Application Program Interface*, specifies the LDAP Version 2 protocol. There is a newer version under way, currently an Internet Draft, specifying LDAP Version 3, which will eventually make RFC 1823 obsolete. The latest version of this draft can be found on the Web site of the Internet Engineering Task Force (IETF), see A.4, "Other Sources" on page 140 for a URL.

There is no RFC available for the Java Naming and Directory Interface (JNDI). JNDI was developed by Sun Microsystems and is supported by many vendors, including Hewlett-Packard, Novell and IBM. Detailed documentation and specifications can be found at `java.sun.com/products/jndi/index.html`.

This chapter is intended to help you get started with LDAP programming. Although the API is not a very complex one—it consists of about 50 distinct function calls. We focus only on the major functions, which are discussed by means of some simple examples. This should help you understand how the API works.

We focus first on the C language API. After concluding the discussion of the API itself, we describe five simple LDAP command line applications that can be used to manage a directory on a basic scale. Next, we turn our attention to LDAP URLs that are defined in RFC 2255, The *LDAP URL Format*. The chapter concludes with a discussion of the Java Naming and Directory Interface (JNDI) to LDAP.

4.1 LDAP Software Development Kits (SDKs)

An LDAP Software Development Kit is a set of libraries and header files. It is
available for a wide variety of operating systems, including several UNIX
platforms and Microsoft Windows. The SDKs most often also include the
command line tools described in 4.3, "LDAP Command Line Tools" on page
115.

There are a number of vendors that offer LDAP directory servers, and thus
also SDKs to enable communication between applications and servers.
Among them are, for example, Netscape and IBM. One SDK that is freely
available on the Internet is from the University of Michigan. Information about
where to find different SDKs can be found in Appendix A, "Other LDAP
References" on page 139.

4.2 The C Language API to LDAP

The following section describes the API library for C language applications.
We use an example-driven approach to discuss the basic functions used for
establishing connections, doing searches and parsing the results. You will
often find the LDAP server *saturn* mentioned in these examples. This is the
name of the LDAP server that was used to run the examples, running the IBM
eNetwork LDAP Directory Server for AIX.

4.2.1 Getting Started

Basic conversation between an LDAP client and an LDAP server is
essentially accomplished in four steps:

- The first step is to initialize an LDAP session. This is done with the
  `ldap_open()` function call, which returns a handle to an LDAP session,
  allowing multiple sessions to be open at once.

- The next step is the authentication to the server. `ldap_simple_bind_s()` and
  related functions are responsible for that. They support various

authentication methods, from simple authentication to the more sophisticated method Simple Authentication and Security Layer (SASL), available in LDAP Version 3.

- Once the connection is successfully established, you can perform your LDAP operation(s), such as searching the directory for information and retrieving the results.

- Finally, the connection has to be closed with the `ldap_unbind()` function call.

Here is a first, simple example that shows these basic steps:

```c
/* example #1
 *   file: just_bind.c
 */

#include <stdio.h>
#include <ldap.h>

main()
{
        LDAP            *ld;
        char            *User = NULL;
        char            *Passwd = NULL;

/* open a connection */
if ((ld = ldap_open("saturn.itso.austin.ibm.com", LDAP_PORT)) == NULL) {
                fprintf(stderr, "ldap_open call failed !");
                exit(1);
}

/* authenticate as nobody */
if (ldap_simple_bind_s(ld, User, Passwd) != LDAP_SUCCESS) {
                ldap_perror(ld, "ldap_simple_bind_s");
                exit(1);
}

/* .............
 *   do something, for example
 *   ask the server for information
 .......... */

/* close and free connection resources */
ldap_unbind(ld);
exit(0);
}
```

The ldap_open() function takes as arguments the name of the LDAP server and the port where it is listening. The symbolic constant, LDAP_PORT, is set in the ldap.h file to 389. This is the default, non-secure port for LDAP. In case of success, ldap_open() returns a pointer to a data structure (a session handle) which contains information about the current session. It must be passed on to subsequent calls that refer to this session. In case of failure, ldap_open() returns NULL.

A look at the access log file of the LDAP server reveals that we have successfully connected (Netscape's Directory Server was used in this example):

```
...
[26/Mar/1998:14:22:42 -0600] conn=172 fd=35 slot=35 connection from 9.3.1.126
[26/Mar/1998:14:22:42 -0600] conn=172 op=0 BIND dn="" method=128 version=2
[26/Mar/1998:14:22:42 -0600] conn=172 op=0 RESULT err=0 tag=97 nentries=0
[26/Mar/1998:14:22:42 -0600] conn=172 op=1 UNBIND
[26/Mar/1998:14:22:42 -0600] conn=172 op=1 fd=35 closed
```

Notice that no user is listed in the dn field of the log file, which indicates that the client is authenticated as user *anonymous*. This is done by passing NULL values as user ID and password to the server within the ldap_simple_bind_s() instruction (see program example above). In case of success, ldap_simple_bind_s() returns LDAP_SUCCESS, an error code is returned otherwise. For more information about error handling, see 4.2.7, "Error Handling" on page 104.

Instead of using ldap_open(), we could have used ldap_init() as well. It takes the same arguments, and it returns the same type of session handle. The difference between these two methods is that ldap_init() does not actually open a connection to the LDAP server. Therefore, you are able to change session settings as defined in the ID structure before the first connection occurs. When using ldap_init(), the first function that actually requires a connection will establish it automatically. In our example above, that would have been the ldap_simple_bind_s() function.

Listed below are some of the session settings you can influence. You can find the complete list of possible options either in the API RFC or in the header file of your SDK:

LDAP_OPT_SIZELIMIT   The maximum number of entries returned in a search; a value of LDAP_NO_LIMIT means no limit.

LDAP_OPT_TIMELIMIT	The maximum number of seconds spent on a search; a value of LDAP_NO_LIMIT means no limit.
LDAP_OPT_DEREF	The way to handle aliases. It can have one of the following values: LDAP_DEREF_NEVER, LDAP_DEREF_SEARCHING, LDAP_DEREF_FINDING, or LDAP_DEREF_ALWAYS. The LDAP_DEREF_SEARCHING means aliases should be dereferenced during the search but not when locating the base object of the search. The LDAP_DEREF_FINDING value means aliases should be dereferenced when locating the base object but not during the search.
LDAP_OPT_REFERRALS	Controls whether the LDAP library automatically follows referrals (LDAP_OPT_ON) or not (LDAP_OPT_OFF).
LDAP_OPT_HOST_NAME	The host name of the default LDAP server.
LDAP_OPT_ERROR_NUMBER	The number of the most recent LDAP error that occurred for this session.
LDAP_OPT_ERROR_STRING	The message returned with the most recent LDAP error that occurred for this session.

The way to set the session preferences depends on the SDK you are using. In IBM's or Netscape's SDKs, the connection handle is an opaque data structure that can only be accessed with the functions

```
int ldap_get_option(
        LDAP            *ld,
        int             option,
        void            *outvalue);
```

and

```
int ldap_set_option(
        LDAP            *ld,
        int             option,
        void            *invalue);
```

Both functions return either LDAP_SUCCESS (integer value of zero) or an nonzero value, and the specified error code is set within the LDAP session handle. The option parameter specifies which session option is to be get or set. The invalue or outvalue parameters contain the new value for the option or the retrieved option value. This is a void pointer because the appropriate type depends on the option chosen. A short example follows for both of these functions.

To check whether or not the client automatically follows referrals returned from the LDAP server (default is yes), the code in the following example (example 2) could be used:

```
/* example #2
 *  file: get_option.c
 */

#include <stdio.h>
#include <ldap.h>

main()
{
        LDAP            *ld;
        int             optdata;
        int             res;

/*open a connection */
if ((ld = ldap_init("saturn.itso.austin.ibm.com", LDAP_PORT))
                == NULL)
                exit(1);

if (ldap_get_option(ld, LDAP_OPT_REFERRALS, &optdata) != LDAP_SUCCESS){
                ldap_perror(ld, "ldap_simple_bind_s");
                exit(1);
                }
else {
        switch(optdata){
                case LDAP_OPT_ON:
                        printf("Follow Referrals is activated\n");break;
                case LDAP_OPT_OFF:
                        printf("Don't Follow Referrals\n");break;

        }
}
exit(0);
}
```

The appropriate option to check is, as listed above, LDAP_OPT_REFERRALS. The
result is captured in the integer variable, optdata, which is checked
subsequently to find out which option is set.

To set the maximum number of seconds spend on each search, the
LDAP_OPT_TIMELIMIT option has to be passed to the ldap_set_option() function:

```
/* Set number of seconds to spend on a search */
max_sec = 60;
if (ldap_set_option(ld, LDAP_OPT_TIMELIMIT,
                (void *)&max_sec) != LDAP_SUCCESS) {
        ldap_perror( ld, "ldap_set_option" );
        exit(1);
}
```

4.2.2 Synchronous and Asynchronous Use of the API

You may have noticed the "_s" at the end of the bind command in example 1 above. This indicates that this command operates in synchronous mode with the LDAP server. We could have used `ldap_simple_bind()` (without a trailing _s) instead; then the communication would have been asynchronous. But what is the difference between the two modes?

The LDAP protocol allows you to handle multiple sessions at the same time. This means that several queries can be on their way to the server, and the order in which they are processed is up to the server. The LDAP protocol itself is therefore an asynchronous protocol.

In synchronous mode, the client sends a request to the server, and the function call only returns when it gets the reply from the server. It is blocked in between, which in fact means that no other operations can be processed. There is no message ID related to the request. The synchronous function returns either success or an appropriate error code.

When the client sends or receives requests in asynchronous mode, every message is tagged with a message ID that is unique for a given session. The client needs to use the function `ldap_result()` to check the status of the request and get the results. The advantage of this approach is that the time gap between sending a request and actually getting the result from the server can be used by the client to do other work.

Figure 27 illustrates the differences between synchronous and asynchronous requests, and code samples are provided for each mode.

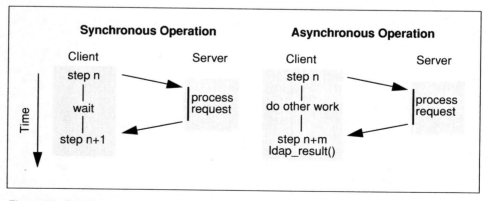

Figure 27. Synchronous Versus Asynchronous Calls

Only functions that actually send data over the network are involved when comparing synchronous versus asynchronous functions. Each of these network-related functions therefore exists in either mode, an appended "_s" indicating the synchronous mode.

The synchronous approach is certainly not as powerful as the asynchronous mode. This means that complex operations with a large number of requests simply take more time. On the other hand, synchronous mode is much simpler to use. The method you chose therefore depends on what you intend to do.

4.2.3 A Synchronous Search Example

So far, our sample application above has only established a connection to an LDAP server, but hasn't actually performed any operations. Now, we go a bit more into details and provide a client that connects to the server and performs a search operation.

```
/* example #3
 *  file: search_and_count.c
 */

#include <stdio.h>
#include <ldap.h>

#define SEARCHBASE      "o=IBM,c=US"

main()
{
        LDAP            *ld;
        LDAPMessage     *res;
        int             numfound;
        char            *User = NULL;
        char            *Passwd = NULL;
        char            line[ BUFSIZ ], search[] = "cn=";

/* Ask for the Name to search for */
printf("Type in a name to search for on LDAP server saturn:\n");
fgets( line, sizeof( line ), stdin );
strcat(search, line);
search[ strlen(search) - 1] = '\0';

/* open a connection */
if ((ld = ldap_open("saturn.itso.austin.ibm.com", LDAP_PORT)) == NULL)
        exit(1);

/* authenticate as nobody */
```

```
if (ldap_simple_bind_s(ld, User, Passwd) != LDAP_SUCCESS) {
        ldap_perror(ld, "ldap_simple_bind_s");
        exit(1);
}

/* search the database */
if (ldap_search_s(ld, SEARCHBASE, LDAP_SCOPE_SUBTREE, search, NULL,
    0, &res) != LDAP_SUCCESS) {
        ldap_perror(ld, "ldap_search_s");
        exit(1);
}

/* did we get anything ? */
if ((numfound = ldap_count_entries(ld, res )) == -1) {
        ldap_perror(ld, "ldap_count_entries");
        exit(1);
}

/* free memory allocated for search results */
ldap_msgfree(res);

/* close and free connection resources */
ldap_unbind(ld);

/* print the results */
printf("Found %d entries of name %s\n\n", numfound, line);
exit(0);


}
```

After asking for a name to search for from the command line, the program connects to saturn, the LDAP server, and searches for that name. The number of hits is then printed to the screen. Keep in mind that you are only able to find an entry if the access control of that entry is set appropriately. Otherwise, the entry may be there, but you are not allowed to search it.

There are three search functions: `ldap_search_s()`, `ldap_search_st()` and `ldap_search()` (two additional functions are mentioned in the API draft for LDAP Version 3, which support controls). The first two functions are used in synchronous mode; the last one provides an asynchronous search function. In addition to the function of `ldap_search()`, `ldap_search_st()` lets you specify a time-out value for each search operation.

In the example above, `ldap_search_s()` was used. Its syntax is:

```
int ldap_search_s(
        LDAP        *ld,
```

```
            char      *base,
            int       scope,
            char      *filter,
            char      **attrs,
            int       attrsonly
);
```

The meaning of the parameters is as follows:

ld   The session handle obtained by `ldap_init()`.

base   A DN which defines the starting point in the LDAP directory tree.

scope   This defines the way how a search in a tree is done. You can choose one of the three possibilities: LDAP_SCOPE_BASE, LDAP_SCOPE_ONELEVEL, LDAP_SCOPE_SUBTREE. See explanation that follows below.

filter   A character string as described in RFC 2254, *The String Representation of LDAP Search Filters*, representing the search filter, as explained in 2.2.3.1, "Search" on page 36.

attrs   A NULL-terminated array of strings indicating which attributes to return for each matching entry. Passing NULL for this parameter causes all available attributes to be retrieved.

attrsonly   A Boolean value that should be zero if both attribute types and values are to be returned, nonzero if only types are wanted. The latter option is useful if, you for example, you want to check to see if only a certain attribute is available.

To search an LDAP directory, a starting point in the tree structure of your directory hierarchy has to be defined. In our example, this is done by setting the base parameter for `ldap_search_s()` to "o=IBM,c=US".

Next, an appropriate scope needs to be chosen. There are three choices for selecting a search scope (see also Figure 28):

- A particular entry (LDAP_SCOPE_BASE) can be searched for.

- The search can be extended to one level below the base, not including the base (LDAP_SCOPE_ONELEVEL).

- The whole subtree under the starting point can be searched (LDAP_SCOPE_SUBTREE).

In the example above, we set scope to subtree (LDAP_SCOPE_SUBTREE) to look for entries containing the common name (cn) typed in by the user on the command line. The common name is appended to the attribute cn which is stored altogether in the variable search. This defines the simple search filter used in the example above. Because the `attrs` parameter is set to NULL and `attrsonly` is set to zero, all attributes with there values are retrieved.

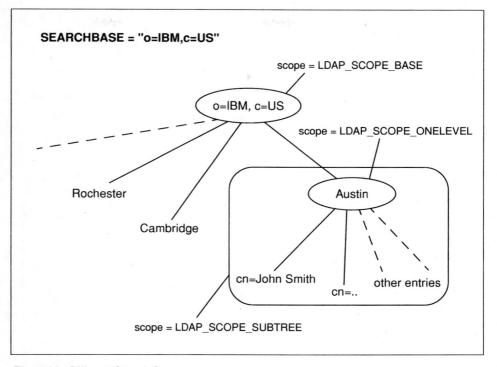

Figure 28. Different Search Scopes

The result of the directory search is returned by `ldap_search_s()` to a structure of type `LDAPMessage` pointed to by the `res` pointer. When no longer needed, the memory allocated in `res` should be freed using `ldap_msgfree()` function (see sample code above). The function `ldap_count_entries()` is then used to count the number of entries found in the directory matching the search filter. Its syntax is:

```
int ldap_count_entries(LDAP *ld, LDAPMessage *result);
```

where `ld` is the connection handle and `result` is a pointer returned to the `LDAPMessage` structure filled by `ldap_search_s()` or `ldap_result()`. In case of an error, `ldap_count_entries()` returns -1, otherwise the number of entries found.

The function `ldap_msgfree(LDAPMessage *result)` should be used to free the memory space occupied by the search results. When successful, the result type freed is returned. This would be `LDAP_RES_SEARCH_ENTRY` in our case.

4.2.4 More about Search Filters

We used the filter `cn=common name` to look up directory entries. But the filter parameter of the search functions is much more flexible. Its syntax is defined in RFC 2254, *The String Representation of LDAP Search Filters.*

The basic syntax of the search filter is as follows:

```
(attribute operator value)
```

So, when we use the filter `cn=John Smith`, cn is the attribute, the equal sign is the operator, and John Smith is the value. There are several more operators available, for example comparison operators like smaller than (<=) or greater than (>=). Furthermore, you can combine several filters using Boolean operators and thus search, for example, for more than one attribute. For a more detailed discussion about search filters and their capabilities, see 2.2.3.3, "Search Filter Syntax" on page 39.

4.2.5 Parsing Search Results

The outcome of a search request is usually a chain of entries, as shown in Figure 29. The last example program only counted the number of entries. But that is usually not what we want; we are interested in the information itself. Therefore we need to parse the information returned by the server. This is an iterative process which starts at the very outside of the data container (an entry) and digs itself deeper in the data structure until it eventually gets to the single attribute/value pairs. The functions we need are:

```
LDAPMessage *ldap_first_entry(LDAP *ld, LDAPMessage *result);
LDAPMessage *ldap_next_entry(LDAP *ld, LDAPMessage *preventry);
```

where:

`ld`	is the connection handle
`result`	is a pointer to the data structure obtained by `ldap_search_s()`, `ldap_search_st()`, or `ldap_result()`
`preventry`	is a pointer to an entry returned by a previous `ldap_first_entry()` or `ldap_next_entry()`
`return value`	if successful, returns a pointer to the first (`ldap_first_entry()`) or to the next entry (`ldap_next_entry()`), or NULL in case of no more entries or an error

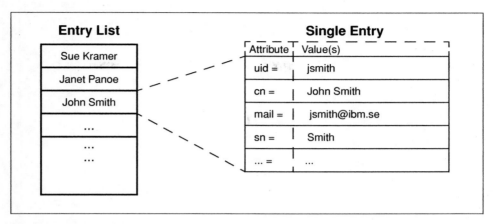

Figure 29. Result of a Search Request

But to actually retrieve the contents of an entry, we need to go further on. As outlined in 2.2.2, "The Naming Model" on page 28, an entry of an LDAP directory consists of attribute/value pairs as defined in the object classes. The following functions retrieve the name of single attributes:

```
char *ldap_first_attribute(LDAP *ld, LDAPMessage *entry, BerElement **ber);
char *ldap_next_attribute(LDAP *ld, LDAPMessage *entry, BerElement *ber);
```

`ld`   is the connection handle

`entry`   is a pointer to an structure returned by `ldap_first_entry()` or `ldap_next_entry()`

`ber`   is a pointer to a data structure which is used to keep track of the current attribute. `BerElement` refers to data encoded using the Basic Encoding Rules. This pointer needs to be passed to subsequent calls of `ldap_next_attribute()`.

Now that we have the attribute names, we are ready for the last step. We can retrieve the attribute values. The function used depends on the attribute types. If they consist of string data, the function

```
char **ldap_get_values(LDAP *ld, LDAPMessage *entry, const char *attr);
```

can be used. If the attribute contains binary data, such as images in JPEG format, we have to use

```
struct berval **ldap_get_values_len(
                  LDAP *ld, LDAPMessage *entry, const char *attr);
```

The parameters ID and entry are the same as in `ldap_first_attribute()` and `ldap_next_attribute()`. The parameter `attr` is a character string returned by `ldap_first_attribute()` and `ldap_next_attribute()`. Example 4 shows a function called `check_result_and_print()` using the functions described above to parse search results:

```c
/* example #4
 *  file f_check_result_and_print.c
 */

#include <stdio.h>
#include <ldap.h>

void check_result_and_print(LDAP *ld, LDAPMessage *res){

LDAPMessage     *entry;
BerElement      *ptr;
int             numfound, i;
char            *dn, *attr, **vals;

/* did we get anything? */
if ((numfound = ldap_count_entries(ld, res)) == -1) {
    ldap_perror(ld, "ldap_count_entries");
    exit(1);
}

/* parse the results */
if (numfound > 0) {

    /* for each entry print out dn plus attributes */
    for (entry = ldap_first_entry(ld,res); entry != NULL;
                        entry = ldap_next_entry(ld,entry)) {

        /* check for distinguished name */
        if((dn = ldap_get_dn(ld,entry)) != NULL){
                printf("\n\ndn: %s\n", dn);
                ldap_memfree(dn);
        }

        /* get the attributes */
        for (attr = ldap_first_attribute(ld, entry, &ptr);
                    attr != NULL;
                    attr = ldap_next_attribute(ld, entry, ptr)) {
            printf("%s: ", attr);

            /* print each value */
            vals = ldap_get_values(ld, entry, attr);
            for (i = 0; vals[i] != NULL; i++) {
            printf("%s, ", vals[i]);
```

```
                    }
                    /* print the end of line for each attr. */
                    printf("\n");
                    ldap_value_free(vals);
              }
       printf("\n");
       }
} else {
    /* print that we didn't get anything */
    printf("Nothing found!\n");
}

/* free the search results */
ldap_msgfree(res);
}
```

This function takes as input the connection handle `ld` and a pointer to a structure `res` as returned by the `ldap_search_s()` function. First, it checks using the `ldap_count_entries()` function what `ldap_search_s()` has returned. Next, if the number of entries is greater than zero, it starts parsing the results.

The attribute/value pairs are printed out in LDIF format as described in 2.4.2, "LDAP Data Interchange Format (LDIF)" on page 50. To be LDIF compliant the first line of every entry has to be the distinguished name (DN). The `ldap_get_dn()` function looks it up for us. Its syntax is:

```
char *ldap_get_dn(LDAP *ld, LDAPMessage *entry);
```

The parameters `ld` and `entry` are the same as in the `ldap_next_entry()` function. After retrieving the DN, we use the function `ldap_memfree()` to free the memory occupied by `ldap_get_dn()`. You may also notice the function `ldap_value_free()`. This is used to free memory blocked by the array which contains the attribute values. Its return value is void.

4.2.6 An Asynchronous Example

So far, we have only dealt with synchronous functions. We now change our search example in order to make it communicate asynchronously with the LDAP server. As mentioned in 4.2.2, "Synchronous and Asynchronous Use of the API" on page 91, the function `ldap_search()` is used for that purpose. It only initiates the search and therefore does not directly return the results. Instead, it returns a message ID which identifies the search being processed by the server and serves as a parameter for the `ldap_result()` function, which can subsequently be used to check the search results.

```
int ldap_search(LDAP *ld, const char *base,
               int scope, const char* filter,
```

```
                     char **attrs, int attrsonly);
```

Note that the pointer to the result structure is missing as a parameter here as compared to the example shown in 4.2.3, "A Synchronous Search Example" on page 92. The other parameters behave like the ones already mentioned as we described `ldap_search_s()`. Here is the example code:

```c
/* example #5
 *  file search_and_parse_async0.c
 */

#include <stdio.h>
#include <string.h>
#include <ldap.h>

#define SEARCHBASE        "o=ibm,c=US"

/* prototype */
void check_result_and_print(LDAP *ld, LDAPMessage *res);

main()
{
        LDAP              *ld;
        LDAPMessage       *res;
        char              *User = NULL;
        char              *Passwd = NULL;
        char              line[BUFSIZ], *filter, temp[BUFSIZ];
        int               msgid, rc,i;
        struct timeval    tv = {0, 0};
strcpy(temp, "cn=");

/* ask for the Name to search for */
printf("\nType in a name to search for on LDAP server saturn:\n");
fgets( line, 20, stdin );
strcat(temp, line);
temp[ strlen(temp) - 1] = '\0';
filter = temp;

/* open a connection */
if ((ld = ldap_open("saturn.itso.austin.ibm.com", LDAP_PORT))
                == NULL)
                exit(1);

/* authenticate as nobody */
if (ldap_simple_bind_s(ld, User, Passwd) != LDAP_SUCCESS) {
                ldap_perror(ld, "ldap_simple_bind_s");
                exit(1);
```

```
        }

        /* search asynchronously */
        if ((msgid = ldap_search(ld, SEARCHBASE, LDAP_SCOPE_SUBTREE,
                    filter, NULL, 0)) == -1){
                ldap_perror(ld, "ldap_search_s");
                exit(1);
        }

        /* Initialize the value returned by ldap_result() */
        rc = 0;
        i = 0;
        while(rc == 0) {

                /* ... do other work */
                        printf("Loopcount %i\n",i++);
                                /* while waiting ... */
                /* check the status of the search operation */
                rc = ldap_result(ld, msgid, 1, &tv, &res);

                switch(rc) {
                    case 0:
                        /* do nothing, search is still in progress */
                        break;
                    case -1:
                        /* some error occurred */
                        ldap_perror(ld, "ldap_result");
                        exit(1);
                        break;

                    case LDAP_RES_SEARCH_RESULT:
                        /* result is complete, print it */
                        check_result_and_print(ld, res);
                        break;
                }
        }

        /* close and free connection resources */
        ldap_unbind(ld);

        exit(0);

}
```

Checking of the search results is done in the `while()` loop using the `ldap_result()` function. This function can be generally used to retrieve results of asynchronous search functions. The return value can have one of three general values. If it is -1, then some sort of error has occurred. A value of zero indicates a time-out, and a value greater than zero indicates a successful returning of a result. The various possible positive return values are declared in the ldap.h file. Only three of these return values are relevant to the search function. The reminder of possible return values belongs to several other asynchronous functions used, for example to add, modify, compare, or delete LDAP tree values. The (positive) return values associated with `ldap_search()` are:

`LDAP_RES_SEARCH_ENTRY`	A single entry matching a previously initiated search result.
`LDAP_RES_SEARCH_RESULT`	Either a result indicating the final outcome of a previously initiated search operation or an entire chain of entries matching a the search operation along with the final outcome.
`LDAP_RES_SEARCH_REFERENCE`	When the search result is a reference, this was added in LDAP Version 3.

For reasons of completeness, here are the other result values. Apart from the last one, the names should be self-explanatory:

- `LDAP_RES_BIND`
- `LDAP_RES_MODIFY`
- `LDAP_RES_ADD`
- `LDAP_RES_DELETE`
- `LDAP_RES_MODDN`
- `LDAP_RES_COMPARE`
- `LDAP_RES_EXTENDED` (new in LDAP Version 3, this is the return of a protocol extensibility operation)

The syntax of `ldap_result()` is:

```
int ldap_result(LDAP *ld, int msgid, int all,
                struct timeval *timeout, LDAPMessage **result);
```

where:

`ld`	The connection handle.
`msgid`	This is the return value of a previously issued asynchronous function, in our case `ldap_search()`. If you specify the constant LDAP_RES_ANY (-1) then the result of any operation is requested.
`all`	Boolean parameter that is only used in search operations. If it is set to zero (false), only one message at a time is retrieved; if it is set to non-zero (true), all results should be received before returning them in a search chain.

`timeout`   A structure which specifies how long to wait for results to be returned. It takes the parameter `tv_sec` and `tv_usec`, which specify seconds and micro seconds of the time interval. A NULL value causes `ldap_result()` not to return until results are available. A zero value (numeric "0", not to confuse with NULL) specifies a polling behavior. This means if values are available, `ldap_result()` retrieves them immediately; if not, it will not wait.

`res`   A pointer to the result obtained by asynchronous operations. This memory area should be freed with `ldap_msgfree()` when it is no longer needed.

Through the setting of the parameter "all" to true in example 5, we specified that we want all results retrieved at once. The time-out period of zero seconds (see the tv structure in the sample code) causes a polling behavior. Therefore, every call of `ldap_result()` checks whether the search operation has already finished. If not, it returns (with value zero in that case) and other work can be done within the while loop. In our case, it simply prints out the number of loops already processed. If `ldap_result()` returns `LDAP_RES_SEARCH_RESULT`, that indicates that the final outcome of the search operation, and the chain of results is available. The result processing is then done by the formerly introduced function (see example 4) `check_result_and_print()`.

As mentioned at the beginning of this section, this is the big advantage of the asynchronous method. Once the asynchronous command is transferred to the server, the client is free to do other things. It uses the `msgid` and `ldap_result()` to check the outcome of the operation whenever appropriate.

We specified in the above example, by setting the parameter "all" to true, that all results should get returned at once. This may be inconvenient, especially when a large number of entries may be expected. In setting the parameter all to false, we can cause `ldap_result()` to deliver single search entries and not the whole result chain. This frees the client from waiting until the complete result chain is available. Every time a new result entry is available, `ldap_return()` delivers `LDAP_RES_SEARCH_ENTRY` as return value instead for of `LDAP_RES_SEARCH_RESULT`. However, the latter value indicates the end of the result list and delivers the final outcome. The following lines change the result processing behavior as just described; the rest of the code is the same as in example 5:

```
/* Initialize the values  */
rc = 0;
i = 0;


/* while the search is still in progress, do this */
```

```
while(rc != LDAP_RES_SEARCH_RESULT) {

    /* ... do other work */
            printf("Loopcount %i\n",i++);
                    /* while waiting ... */
    /* check the status of the search operation */
    rc = ldap_result(ld, msgid, 0, &tv, &res );

    switch(rc) {
        case -1:
            /* some error occurred */
            ldap_perror(ld, "ldap_result");
            exit( 1 );
            break;
        case LDAP_RES_SEARCH_ENTRY:
            check_result_and_print(ld, res);
            break;
        case 0:
            /* no result yet */
            break;
    }
}
```

4.2.7 Error Handling

If an LDAP function fails, information about what went wrong can be found in the connection handle. Most of the error codes, which go into three separate fields of the connection handle, are directly returned from the server, but the fields can get set from client library functions as well. The fields are:

ld_matched   In the event of an LDAP_NO_SUCH_OBJECT error, this parameter contains the part of the DN that could be matched with a DN found on the server.

ld_error   This parameter contains the error message sent in the result by the server.

ld_errno   The LDAP error code like LDAP_SUCCESS, LDAP_NO_SUCH_OBJECT, LDAP_STRONG_AUTH_REQUIRED, and so forth. indicating the outcome of the operation.

How the error processing works depends on what LDAP function you use. Most functions (all synchronous functions) directly return numerical error codes. They can get mapped by the function ldap_err2string() to character strings which in turn can get printed to standard error output or to whatever is convenient for you.

When, for example, searching the directory server using the synchronous function `ldap_search_s()`, the error checking can be done like this:

```
/* search the database */
if ((rc = ldap_search_s(ld, SEARCHBASE, LDAP_SCOPE_SUBTREE, search, NULL,
                        0, &res)) != LDAP_SUCCESS){
        fprintf(stderr, "ldap_search_s: %s\n", ldap_err2string(rc));
        exit(1);
}
```

In case of success, `ldap_search_s()` returns `LDAP_SUCCESS` (which is equivalent to zero) or the appropriate numerical error code. If we set the `SEARCHBASE` parameter to a nonexistent value, for example `o=icm,c=us` instead of `o=ibm,c=us`, then the error message of the previous example would be as follows (the particular return code equals to 32, `LDAP_NO_SUCH_OBJECT`):

```
ldap_search_s: No such object
```

This indicates that the entry we were looking for does not exist, either due to an incorrect DN or for other reasons. For your reference, C.2, "LDAP API Error Codes" on page 158, lists all error codes that are used in the LDAP API calls.

A common way to monitor the return code of an LDAP function for errors is also to use the function `void ldap_perror(LDAP *ld, char *msg)`. In fact, as you might have noticed, that is what we did in our examples so far. This function was defined in the LDAP Version 2 API. It internally converts the error contained in the `ld_errno` field of the session handle to an error string and prints it together with the `msg` string to standard error (stderr). In the LDAP Version 3 API draft, the use of this function is deprecated. Therefore, using the `ldap_err2string()` function should be the preferred way in LDAP Version 3.

When checking for an error of an asynchronous function, `ldap_parse_result()` has to be used. This is because the function that checks the outcome of the operation, `ldap_result()`, returns the type of the result (for example `LDAP_RES_ADD`, `LDAP_RES_SEARCH_ENTRY`, and so on) instead of the LDAP error code.

The routine `ldap_parse_result()` checks messages of type `LDAP_RES_SEARCH_ENTRY` and `LDAP_RES_SEARCH_REFERENCE` returned from the LDAP server when looking for a result message to parse. It returns the constant `LDAP_SUCCESS` if the result was successfully parsed and no error was found; otherwise it returns another error code. This function then also sets the appropriate fields in the connection handle. The syntax of `ldap_parse_result()` is as follows:

```
int ldap_parse_result(LDAP            *ld,
                       LDAPMessage     *res,
                       int             *errcodep,
                       char            **matcheddnp,
                       char            **errmsgp,
                       char            ***referralsp,
                       LDAPControl     ***serverctrlsp,
                       int             freeit);
```

The parameters are:

ld, res
: The connection file handle and the pointer to the message structure which contains the result of an LDAP operation, as returned by ldap_result().

errcodep
: An integer pointer that will be filled with the error code of the LDAP operation. That is the way the server tells the client about the outcome of its operation. NULL may be passed to ignore this field.

matcheddnp
: In case of an LDAP_NO_SUCH_OBJECT error, this parameter will be filled with the part of the distinguished name that could be matched. NULL may be passed to ignore this field. The memory area occupied by this parameter should be freed using the ldap_memfree() command.

errmsgp
: This result parameter will be filled in with the contents of the error message contained in the returned message. NULL may be passed to ignore this field. The memory area occupied by this parameter should be freed using the ldap_memfree() command.

referralsp
: This parameter will be filled in with the contents of the referrals field contained in the returned message, indicating zero or more alternate LDAP servers where the information should be retrieved. The referrals array should be freed by calling ldap_value_free(). NULL may be passed to ignore this field.

serverctrlsp
: This result parameter will be filled in with an allocated array of controls copied out of the LDAPMessage structure. The occupied memory area should be freed using ldap_controls_free().

freeit
: This determines whether or not the LDAPMessage structure is cleared after extracting the necessary information. Pass a nonzero value to free it.

Note that ldap_parse_result() places the error code in the errcodep parameter. Thus, check this parameter to trace errors of previous LDAP operations.

If we apply this to our last example, the asynchronous search example, we could do the following the check for errors after the `ldap_search()` has been invoked (the complete code sample can be found in the file search_and_parse_async_errv3.c):

```
/* while the search is still in progress, do this */
while(rc != LDAP_RES_SEARCH_RESULT ) {

        /* ... do other work */
            printf("Loopcount %i\n",i++);
                    /* while waiting ... */
        /* check the status of the search operation */
        rc = ldap_result(ld, msgid, 0, &tv, &res );
        switch(rc) {
            case -1:
                /* some error occurred */
                fprintf(stderr, "ldap_search_s: %s\n", ldap_err2string(rc));
                exit(1);
                break;
            case LDAP_RES_SEARCH_ENTRY:
                check_result_and_print(ld, res);
                break;

            /* this is the end of the search, test for errors */
            case LDAP_RES_SEARCH_RESULT:
                ldap_parse_result(ld,res,&err,&errdn,&errmsg,NULL,NULL,1);
                if ( err != LDAP_SUCCESS) {
                        fprintf(stderr,
                            "Search Error: %s, %s, Matched DN:%s\n",
                            errmsg, ldap_err2string(err), errdn);
                        ldap_memfree(errdn);
                        ldap_memfree(errmsg);
                }
                break;
            case 0:
                /* no result yet */
                break;
        }
}
```

As we pointed out earlier, when the `all` parameter in `ldap_result()` is set to zero (false), single search results get retrieved at a time. The final outcome is stored in the message structure when `LDAP_RES_SEARCH_RESULT` is returned. The function mentioned above, `ldap_parse_result()`, is then used to check the final outcome of the search. The error code is stored in the integer value *err*. A return value not equal to zero (`LDAP_SUCCESS`) indicates a search error. In that case, `ldap_err2string()` is used to transform the error number to the related error string. This is, together with `errmsg` and `matcheddn`, then printed out to the standard error output. `ldap_memfree()` eventually frees no longer needed memory areas.

If we searched for an entry with the same wrong searchbase as in an earlier example above (`o=icm,c=us`), we would get the error message:

```
Search Error: , No such object, Matched DN:c=us
```

This corresponds to an `LDAP_NO_SUCH_OBJECT` error. The errmsg field is not set, but the matched DN field shows us the portion of the name which could successfully be matched.

Two more functions for error checking are mentioned in the LDAP Version 3 API specification. They are called `ldap_parse_sasl_bind()` and `ldap_parse_extended_result()`. The first one is to check for errors resulting from a SASL bind operation; the latter one can be used to check the outcome of extended operations that provide a mechanism in LDAP Version 3 to extend the protocol. For more information about them, we refer you to the LDAP Version 3 API draft itself.

4.2.8 Authentication Methods

Authentication can be understood as identifying the client to the server. This needs to be done before any operation can be performed with the server. There are several authentication mechanism supported in LDAP. We start with Basic Authentication which is, as already discussed in section 2.3.2, "Basic Authentication" on page 44, not actually very secure.

A common way to gain a higher level of security, especially when exchanging information over the Internet, is to use SSL to encrypt the session. As pointed out in 2.3, "Security" on page 43, some vendors of LDAP directory products have extended the API to allow SSL sessions between LDAP servers and clients.

LDAP Version 3 also introduced the SASL authentication framework. We will discuss the bind function call and its parameters to initiate an SASL session. For further reading, please browse the literature listed in A.4, "Other Sources" on page 140.

For general information about the different security techniques and the definitions and terms used below, we refer you to Section 2.3, "Security" on page 43.

If you not only want to read and search a directory but also want to modify the entries in it, the anonymous user authentication used so far to search the directory will certainly not work. You need to authenticate as a user with special access permissions, for example as an authorized directory administrator. Then you are allowed to do modifications (provided the authorization schema is set up correctly). The easiest way to do that is to use basic authentication. This is done by specifying a DN and a password in the `ldap_simple_bind()` function and sending it over to the LDAP server, as in the following example:

```
/* example #6
 *  file: basic_auth.c
 */

#include <stdio.h>
#include <ldap.h>

main()
{
        LDAP            *ld;
        char            *User = "cn=Directory Manager";
        char            *Passwd = "1234qwer";

/* open a connection */
if ((ld = ldap_open("saturn.itso.austin.ibm.com", LDAP_PORT)) == NULL)
                exit(1);

/* authenticate as nobody */
if (ldap_simple_bind_s(ld, User, Passwd) != LDAP_SUCCESS) {
                ldap_perror(ld, "ldap_simple_bind_s");
                exit(1);
}

/* .............
 *  do something, for example
 *  ask the server for information
 ................ */

printf("Authenticated as %s\n", User);

/* close and free connection resources */
ldap_unbind(ld);
exit(0);
}
```

This is the LDAP server's access log file entry after the program above has been run (Netscape's Directory Server):

```
...
[26/Mar/1998:14:12:10 -0600] conn=169 fd=32 slot=32 connection from 9.3.1.126
[26/Mar/1998:14:12:10 -0600] conn=169 op=0 BIND dn="cn=Directory Manager" method=128
version=2
[26/Mar/1998:14:12:10 -0600] conn=169 op=0 RESULT err=0 tag=97 nentries=0
[26/Mar/1998:14:12:10 -0600] conn=169 op=1 UNBIND
[26/Mar/1998:14:12:10 -0600] conn=169 op=1 fd=32 closed
```

Compared to the log in example #1 (shown on page 88), the DN field in the log file is now set to cn=Directory Manager. This solution grants the client the appropriate access permissions. However, as stated before, it is not very secure because the password is sent over the network using a relatively weak encryption technique. A common way to circumvent this security exposure is to use SSL to encrypt your session.

Example #7 shows how to connect to an IBM eNetwork LDAP server using the SSL instructions from IBM's SDK. Prior to using SSL, a public/private key pair and a certificate for your server are needed. For this purpose, IBM ships with its server the mkkf utility to manage keyfiles and certificates.

The following example uses *Server Authentication* only, although the IBM product supports *Client Authentication* as well. When using server authentication, the server proves its identity to the client through a certificate issued by a Certificate Authority, but no client certificate is needed in this case. The client needs to add the server's certificate to his own keyring file and mark it as trusted. We refer you to the IBM *eNetwork LDAP Directory Server Administration Guide* for detailed information on how to set up server security. The creation of keyring files for both client and server is described there as well.

```
/* example #7
 *  file: ssl_auth_dss.c
 */

#include <stdio.h>
#include <ldap.h>

main()
{
        LDAP            *ld;
```

```
        char            *User = "cn=admin,o=ibm,c=us";
        char            *Passwd = "Admin";
        char            *keyring = "/home/root/keys/venus-keyfile.kyr";
        char            *keyring_pw = NULL, *name = NULL;
        int             rc;

/* open a connection */
if ((ld = ldap_open("saturn.itso.austin.ibm.com", LDAPS_PORT)) == NULL){
                perror("ldap_open error");
                exit(1);
}else{
        printf("ldap_open done, %i\n", LDAPS_PORT);
}


rc = ldap_ssl_start(ld, keyring, keyring_pw, name);
if (rc < 0) {
        printf("rc ldap_ssl_start %d\n",  rc);
        exit(1);
}else{
        printf("Success: ldap_ssl_start\n");
}


/* authenticate as admin */
if (ldap_simple_bind_s(ld, User, Passwd) != LDAP_SUCCESS) {
                ldap_perror(ld, "ldap_simple_bind_s");
                exit(1);
}

/* .............
 *   do something, for example
 *   ask the server for information
 ............... */

printf("Authenticated as %s\n", User);

/* close and free connection resources */
ldap_unbind(ld);
exit(0);
}
```

The first difference to example #6 is that the `ldap_open()` statement initializes
a connection on port `LDAPS_PORT` instead of `LDAP_PORT`. This constant,
`LDAPS_PORT`, is set in the ldap.h file to 636, which is the default SSL port for
LDAP. The actual SSL connection is established using the `ldap_ssl_start()`
function. This command does the SSL negotiation which ends in the

exchange of secret keys to secure the data connection. It takes as input parameters:

ld   The connection handle returned by `ldap_open()`.

keyring   This specifies the name of the keyring file. It usually contains the certificates of the trusted (by the client) Certificate Authorities. It can also contain a public key and the associated certificate. This is only needed when client authentication is required.

keyring_pw   The password which protects the keyring file. It is set when the keyring file is created with the `mkkf` tool. A NULL password, as in our example, is accepted.

name   When creating your private key/certificate pair with `mkkf`, a label is assigned. This is the name of this label. In our example, we also passed a NULL value here because no client key is involved.

`ldap_ssl_start()` returns an integer less than zero when an error has occurred. If it returns zero, the SSL session is established and data subsequently transferred over the network is encrypted. Therefore it is now safe to send user ID and password with the `ldap_simple_bind_s()` command. We run the IBM eNetwork LDAP server in debug mode to monitor the connection. The following output shows the details of this connection:

```
...
New connection identified as SSL connection.
Connection received from 9.3.1.126 on socket 10.
do_bind
Bind operation requested by: cn=admin,o=ibm,c=us.
=> dn_normalize "cn=admin,o=ibm,c=us"
<= dn_normalize "cn=admin,o=ibm,c=us"
do_bind:conn 14 version 2 dn (cn=admin,o=ibm,c=us) method 128
entering rdbm_back_bind...
send_ldap_result 0::
do_unbind conn=14 op=1 fd=12
```

Notice the SSL request before the actual bind occurs.

A very general authentication command available with LDAP Version 3, which offers access to different authentication methods, is the `ldap_sasl_bind_s()` function (or its asynchronous version `ldap_sasl_bind()`). Its syntax is:

```
int ldap_sasl_bind_s(LDAP          *ld,
                     char          *dn,
```

```
char          *mechanism,
struct berval *cred,
LDAPControl   **serverctrls,
LDAPControl   **clientctrls,
struct berval **servercredp );
```

In principle, the SASL functions can be understood as a general authentication framework for the LDAP client. They take as arguments - among others - the DN (the name of the entry to bind as), the mechanism (authentication method) and the credentials used to authenticate. The format of the credentials passed to the SASL command depends on the mechanism used. If the special constant, LDAP_SASL_SIMPLE, is passed, then basic authentication is requested. This is equivalent to using ldap_simple_bind() (or ldap_simple_bind_s()). Other methods, such as Kerberos or S/Key, can be used as well.

SSL, or more general its successor TLS (Transport Layer Security), can get integrated within the SASL Framework through its EXTERNAL mechanism. When this method is chosen and the cred field is empty, the server determines the client's identity through external information. This could be an SSL client certificate issued for the distinguished name used in the ldap_sasl_bind() function to bind to the LDAP server. If the cred field is not empty, the LDAP server has to verify that the client's authenticated TLS credentials allow use of the credentials passed to ldap_sasl_bind().

4.2.9 Multithreaded Applications

Until now, we have only dealt with the single-threaded model of the LDAP API. This was the only model available for LDAP applications using the LDAP Version 2 API. Sometimes you may be in the need for better performance, for example when you try to update a huge amount of directory entries or when your application uses multiple threads anyway. For this purpose, several vendors started to implement there own multithreaded libraries for LDAP. In an effort to overcome such vendor-dependent approaches, the LDAP Version 3 C-language specification has been extended with a common set of multithreaded function calls.

As an example, let's assume that a large number of directory entries have to be modified for some reason. This can, of course, be done by sequentially stepping through the list of entries that have to be modified and doing the changes one after the other. The list will have to be composed first, for example by performing an adequate search.

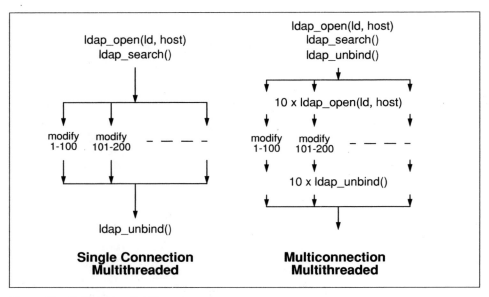

Figure 30. Multiple Parallel Threads

One way to accomplish the modifications is to divide the list of entries into, for example, 10 equal sized blocks. Then you could open multiple connections to your server (issuing `ldap_open()` multiple times), each one running in its own thread, using the multithreading facilities of the operating system. Every thread would obtain its own connection handle for its connection. Every connection handle contains information about the connection itself, fields for error handling, and so on. This results in a multithreaded, multiconnection application, as depicted in Figure 30.

The single connection approach would be to use only one connection but several threads operating on it. Because one connection means only one connection handle, the LDAP Version 3 C API supports functions to isolate information that is vital for each thread, protecting it from getting tampered with by functions from another thread. This is, for example, done by creating thread-specific fields in the connection handle for error handling. Here, the error code of the last instruction issued within the attached thread is stored. Only functions within the same thread can access and evaluate it.

This brief discussion about multithreaded application programming in LDAP Version 3 concludes the introduction to building LDAP-enabled applications. There is, of course, a lot more to it, but it would be beyond the scope of this book to elaborate more on the complete LDAP API and LDAP programming techniques. We refer to A.4, "Other Sources" on page 140, for more references to the subject if you are interested. Also, you should bear in mind that, at the time this book was written, the LDAP Version 3 C language interface was only described in an Internet Draft. Changes are still possible, although not very likely.

For the sake of completeness and for your reference, C.1, "C Language API Calls" on page 153, provides a categorized list of all LDAP C language API calls, with a short description of each.

4.3 LDAP Command Line Tools

Most SDKs come with a set of simple command line applications, either in source code or as ready-to-use executable programs. These tools were built using the LDAP API functions and thus can serve as sample applications. They enable you to do basic operations, such as searching the directory and adding, modifying, or deleting entries within the LDAP server. Each basic operation is accomplished with a single program:

- `ldapsearch`
- `ldapadd`
- `ldapmodify`
- `ldapdelete`
- `ldapmodrdn`

These are their names in a UNIX environment. If you work with a DOS/Windows operating system, the names of the tools end in ".EXE" and may follow an 8.3 file-naming convention. Each utility corresponds to an LDAP protocol operation; only the compare tool is missing. By combining these tools, using for example a scripting language like Perl, you can easily build up more complex applications. In addition, they are easily deployable in Web-based CGI programs.

This section describes the utilities provided with the IBM SDK. With very few exceptions, such as SSL, tools provided by other vendors should work similarly. As this book provides only an overview, we do not discuss all the options of the tools here, just the most common ones. For a detailed description, we refer you to the individual SDK's documentation.

In the following examples, the backslash character ("\") at the end of a line represents a line continuation character because it is common in the UNIX command shell environment.

4.3.1 The Search Tool: ldapsearch

`ldapsearch` is a command line interface to the `ldap_search()` API function and thus allows you to search the directory of an LDAP server. Among other things, you can specify options like `searchbase`, `scope` (`subtree` is default), `filter` and the attributes of the entry you would like to retrieve. The result is printed to standard output. Assume we want to search on an LDAP server, saturn, for entries of John Smith, but we are only interested in the attributes `cn` and `telephonenumber`. The following command would deliver the desired results:

```
ldapsearch -h saturn -b "ou=austin,o=ibm,c=us" -s sub cn="john smith" \
cn telephonenumber
```

This might be the answer we get:

```
cn=John Smith, ou=Austin, o=IBM, c=US
cn=John Smith
telephonenumber=1-512-838-6004
```

The general syntax of `ldapsearch` is:

```
ldapsearch [-options] filter [attributes]
```

In the example above, the following options were used:

-h ldaphost   This is the hostname of the LDAP server.

-b basesearch   Specifies the starting point for the search, in our case `"ou=austin,o=ibm,c=us"`.

-s scope   Specifies the scope of the search: one of `base` (base object search), `one` (one level search) or `sub` (sub tree search) which is the default setting.

For the search filter, the example uses cn="John Smith". This is a simple filter example; more sophisticated combinations of filter strings, for example the combination of different filters using a Boolean operator, are possible, too. See also 2.2.3.1, "Search" on page 36, for more details about search filters.

When no attributes are listed on the right-hand side of the instruction, all available attributes will get retrieved. Otherwise, when several attributes are explicitly stated, only these are returned.

Other useful flags and parameters for the `ldapsearch` tool are:

-v   Verbose mode. This might help to detect some problem because many diagnostic messages are written to standard output.

-A	Retrieves only the attributes, not the values. This can be used when you just want to check whether or not an attribute is present.
-L	Presents the output in LDIF format.
-R	Specifies that referrals are not automatically followed.
-t	Write retrieved values to a set of temporary files. This is especially important when retrieving binary data such as JPEG picture images.
-p ldapport	Specify an alternative port when your server does not listen on the default port.
-l timelimit	Wait not more than timelimit seconds for the search to complete.
-z sizelimit	Do not retrieve more than sizelimit entries.

When you want to retrieve binary data, printing them to standard output is probably a bad idea. The `ldapsearch` utility therefore supports the `-t` option, which allows you to write data into a file. Assume we issue the command:

```
ldapsearch -t -h saturn -b "o=ibm,c=us" "uid=jsmith" jpegPhoto
```

The `ldapsearch` will then print the file name where the value of the attribute `jpegPhoto` has been written to:

```
cn=John Smith, ou=Austin, o=IBM, c=US
jpegPhoto=/tmp/ldap-search-jpegPhoto-a19924
```

4.3.2 The ldapmodify and ldapadd Utilities

These tools present interfaces to the API function calls `ldap_modify()` and `ldap_add()`. Because the functionality of the `ldap_add()` API call is included in `ldap_modify()`, the same is valid for the command line utilities. They differ therefore only in one respect; this is the `-a` (for add) option, which is by default set when you invoke `ldapadd`. The default for `ldapmodify` is to modify existing entries.

The general syntax of the `ldapadd` and `ldapmodify` tools is:

```
ldap{add|modify} [-options] [-f filename]
```

Information about what should be added to or changed in the directory can be retrieved from a file in LDIF format using the -f parameter. The LDIF file format is described in 2.4.2, "LDAP Data Interchange Format (LDIF)" on page 50. If no file is specified, ldapadd and ldapmodify expect attribute/value pairs entered from the command line, Ctrl-C exits the input mode. The most common options are:

-a	Add new entries. This flag is set by default when invoking `ldapadd`.

-b	Assume that the values beginning with a "/" are the pathnames to binary values.
-r	Replace existing values by default.
-n	Show what would be done, but does not actually modify entries.
-v	Verbose mode, write diagnostic messages to standard out.
-R	Specifies that referrals are not be automatically followed.
-D binddn	Use binddn to bind to the LDAP server.
-w passwd	Use passwd for Basic Authentication.
-h ldaphost	Name of the LDAP server that hosts your directory information.
-p ldapport	Port where the LDAP server is listening if it is not the default port 389.

To change, for example John Smith's phone number, you could create an LDIF file named mod.ldif containing the information:

```
dn: cn=John Smith, ou=austin,o=ibm,c=us
telephonenumber: 1-812-838-6004
```

and then issue the command:

```
ldapmodify -R -D "cn=admin,o=ibm,c=us" -w Admin -h saturn -r -f mod.ldif
```

This will change John Smith's entry as desired. We authenticated to the LDAP server as cn=admin.

4.3.3 The ldapdelete Tool

The ldapdelete tool provides an interface to the ldap_delete() API call. Entries with the dn specified are deleted. Its general syntax is:

```
ldapdelete [-options] dn dn ....
```

If no dn is provided, a list of DNs is read form the standard input. Some of the possible options are:

-n	Just list what would happen without actually doing it.
-v	Verbose mode for debugging information.
-R	Do not follow referrals.
-D binddn	Bind to the directory server as binddn.
-w passwd	Use passwd to go with binddn during bind operation.
-h ldaphost	LDAP server is running on ldaphost.
-p ldapport	LDAP server is listening on ldapport.

The command

```
ldapdelete -h saturn -D "Directory Manager" -w passwd "cn=John Smith,\
ou=austin,o=ibm,c=us"
```

would delete John Smith's entry in the directory.

4.3.4 The ldapmodrdn Tool

This tool modifies the Relative Distinguished Name (RDN) of entries. It corresponds to the `ldap_mordn2()` function and gets its input information either from the standard input from a file through the use of the `-f` option or from command line parameters.

```
ldapmodrdn [-options] -f file | olddn newdn
```

Possible options are:

-r	Removes old RDN entry; default is to keep the old one.
-n,-v,-R,-D,-w,-h,-p	Same meaning as options from `ldapdelete`.

For example, to modify the name of the entry "Old One" to "New One", the following lines could be put in an LDIF file called mod.ldif:

```
cn=Old One,o=Austin,ou=IBM,c=US
cn=New One
```

To issue the change, this command must be run:

```
ldapmodrdn -r -D "Directory Manager" -w passwd -f mod.ldif
```

This will modify the RDN accordingly from cn=Old One,o=Austin,ou=IBM,c=US to cn=New One,o=Austin,ou=IBM,c=US and will also remove the old entry dn=Old One,o=Austin,ou=IBM,c=US.

4.3.5 Security Considerations

In the examples above, a distinguished name (DN) and a password were sent over the network to the LDAP server to authenticate the client (or the user, if you will). As mentioned before, this does not provide a high level of security because the information is not really encrypted when sent over the wire and thus could get eavesdropped. Therefore the command line tools mentioned in the previous sections support an SSL mode, which assumes, of course, that the server has its SSL port enabled and SSL is properly enabled and configured.

The options which influence the SSL behavior of the command line tools included in IBM's SDK are:

-Z	Enables secure SSL connection to the LDAP server. This is only supported by SSL versions of the tools. If Z is not set, the options below are ignored.

-K keyfile	Specifies the name and location of the keyring file. The name must be full qualified if it is not in the actual directory. The keyring file must at least contain the certificate of the LDAP server. This enables the server to prove its identity to the client through *server authentication*. If the certificate is self-signed, it must be marked as trustworthy in the client's keyring file. Key and certificate management can be done using the `mkkf` tool, which comes within the SDK from IBM.
-P keyfilepw	The keyring password required to access the information stored in the keyring file.
-N label	This is only required when using *client authentication* in addition to *server authentication*. The label is associated with a client certificate stored in your keyring file and therefore tells the client which certificate it should use to authenticate to the LDAP server. This is only needed when there is more than one Certificate/private key pair or if you do not want to use the default certificate/private key pair.

A Word About Compatibility

Since different vendors might support SSL in different ways, please refer to your SDK's documentation to verify if and how your command line tools can be used in conjunction with the SSL security mechanism.

4.4 LDAP URLs

Uniform Resource Locators (URLs) provide a standard way to refer to resources on the Internet or within an intranet. The most common example is a Web page such as `http://www.ibm.com/Products/index.html`. In this case, `http` refers to the hypertext transfer protocol (HTTP) used by Web browsers, `www.ibm.com` is the host to contact, and `Products/index.html` is the name of a file on that host. Using this URL, a Web browser can retrieve and display the page. URLs are also defined for other protocols such as the File Transfer Protocol (FTP). For example, the URL `ftp://ds.internic.net/rfc/rfc2255.txt` can be used to retrieve the file `/rfc/rfc2255.txt` from the host `ds.internic.net`.

Since LDAP has become an important protocol on the Internet, a URL format for LDAP resources has also been defined. *The LDAP URL Format* (RFC 2255) describes the format of the LDAP URL. LDAP URLs begin with `ldap://` or `ldaps://` if the LDAP server communicates using SSL. LDAP URLs can simply name an LDAP server, or can specify a complex directory search. As we discuss in 4.4.1, "Uses of LDAP URLs" on page 122, LDAP URLs can be used for a number of purposes such as referrals to other LDAP servers or construction of an e-mail distribution list.

The syntax of an LDAP URL is:

```
ldap[s]://[<host>[:<port>]] [/ [<dn> [? [<attributes>] [? [<scope>] \
[? [<filter>] [? <extensions>]]]]]]
```

where:

ldap[s]   ldap specifies a connection using the LDAP protocol, and ldaps specifies an SSL LDAP connection.

host   The name or IP address of the LDAP server host. Host and port can be omitted when used with the LDAP URL APIs described in 4.4.2, "LDAP URL APIs" on page 123.

port   Port number of the LDAP server. The port number defaults to the standard port numbers 389 for LDAP and 636 for LDAPS.

dn   The distinguished name used as the base of the search.

attributes   A comma-separated list of the attributes to return from the search. If none are specified, all attributes are returned.

scope   The scope of the search, one of base, one, or sub. The default is base.

filter   The search filter to apply. If the search filter is omitted, objectClass=*, which returns all entries, is used.

extensions   Allows extensions to the LDAP URL to be defined.

Some examples will help make the format of LDAP URLs clear.

```
ldap://saturn.itso.austin.ibm.com/
```

Refers to the LDAP server on the host saturn.itso.austin.ibm.com, using the default port 389.

```
ldap://saturn.itso.austin.ibm.com:389/o=Transarc,c=US
```

Retrieves all the attributes for the DN o=Transarc,c=US from the LDAP server on host saturn.itso.austin.ibm.com. Note that the port 389 is explicitly specified here as an example. Since 389 is the default port, it would not have been necessary to specify it in the URL.

```
ldap://saturn.itso.austin.ibm.com/cn=John%20Smith,ou=Austin,o=IBM,c=US
```

Retrieves all the attributes for the DN cn=John Smith,ou=Austin,o=IBM,c=US. Note that some characters are considered unsafe in URLs because they can be removed or treated as delimiters by some programs. Unsafe characters such as space, comma, brackets, and so forth. should be represented by their hexadecimal value preceded by the percent sign. In this example, %20 is a space. More information about unsafe characters and URLs in general can be found in *Uniform Resource Locators (URL)* (RFC 1738).

```
ldap://saturn.itso.austin.ibm.com/o=Transarc,c=US??sub?cn=*smith*
```

This URL retrieves all attributes of any entry in the subtree starting at o=Transarc,c=US with a common name attribute that contains the character string smith.

```
ldap://saturn.itso.austin.ibm.com/o=Transarc,c=US?cn,mail,phoneNumber?\
sub?cn=*brown*
```

This is similar to the above example, but it only returns the attributes common name, e-mail address, and phone number.

```
ldap://saturn.itso.austin.ibm.com/o=Transarc,c=US?objectClass?one??\
bindname=cn=John%20Smith%2ou=Austin%2o=Transarc%2c=US
```

This example retrieves the `objectClass` attribute for all objects one level below o=Transarc,c=US. It also illustrates the use of the LDAP URL extension field. The only standard extension defined to date is the DN used to bind to the LDAP server. In this case, the DN `cn=John Smith,ou=Austin,o=Transarc,c=US` is used. The keyword `bindname` can be preceded by ! if the server must support the extension. Otherwise, the server is free to ignore the extension. Extensions are a recent addition to the LDAP URL and might not be supported by some products.

4.4.1 Uses of LDAP URLs

LDAP URLs are very flexible. They can specify anything from an LDAP server to a single attribute of a single directory entry and therefore offer much of the functionality otherwise provided by the API functions. One common use of LDAP URLs is in referrals. As outlined in 2.2.3.2, "Referrals and Continuation References" on page 38, when an LDAP server does not store some part of the directory name space, it can refer to another LDAP server that does. For example, if a server does not store information for the subtree `o=Transarc,c=US`, it can define a directory entry of object class referral for the DN `o=Transarc,c=US`. This object would have a `ref` attribute that contains a URL for an LDAP server that stores information about Transarc. For example, `ref=ldap://gulftower.transarc.com/o=Transarc,c=US`.

LDAP servers can also have a default reference that is used to point to a superior (higher in the name tree) server for any names that cannot be resolved. For example, `ldap://whitepages.ibm.com` could be the default referral for all LDAP servers in IBM if it was at the root of the IBM directory tree.

LDAP URLs can also be used by applications. For example, an e-mail or address book client could store a distribution list as an LDAP URL. The URL `ldap://austin.ibm.com/ou=Austin,o=IBM,c=US?mail?sub?deptartment=itso` retrieves a list of e-mail addresses of people in the ITSO department at IBM in Austin. An LDAP-enabled mail client could even store this URL in the LDAP directory. As people enter and leave the ITSO department, the list is automatically kept up to date because it is created dynamically as the result of an LDAP search on the `department` attribute. It is not a separate list that has to be updated each time a person enters or leaves the department.

Many Web browsers also support browsing resources specified as LDAP URLs. A sophisticated user could enter a complex LDAP URL search, and the results would be displayed by the browser. Entering LDAP URLs directly might not be for everybody, but it can be useful for experimentation and debugging or for arbitrary ad hoc queries. This is similar to entering interactive SQL commands rather than using a database forms application.

Methods are also being discussed within the IETF for storing LDAP URLs in the Domain Name System (DNS). DNS is used to resolve host names to IP addresses and to locate servers, such as mail servers, for a domain. A user who wants to search IBM's publicly accessible LDAP directory would look up the domain ibm.com in the DNS. The DNS entry for ibm.com would contain one or more LDAP server host names. These hosts could then be contacted to execute an LDAP search.

4.4.2 LDAP URL APIs

As discussed above, many applications will need to be aware of LDAP URLs. In some cases, an LDAP server can return a referral back to a client rather than an actual search or read result. Referrals are in the form of an LDAP URL. Or an application such as an e-mail client or address book may manage data in the form of an LDAP URL and hide this representation from the user.

Although they are not included in the IETF RFCs and draft documents, most LDAP SDKs include a set of functions for handling LDAP URLs. The functions listed in Table 15 allow a program to test if a string is an LDAP URL, break the

LDAP URL into its component parts, and use the LDAP URL to perform a search.

Table 15. LDAP URL APIs

Function	Description
ldap_is_ldap_url()	Determines if a string is an LDAP URL.
ldap_url_parse()	Breaks an LDAP URL into its component pieces.
ldap_free urldesc()	Frees memory allocated by `ldap_url_parse()`.
ldap_url_search()	Performs an asynchronous search as specified by the LDAP URL.
ldap_url_search_s()	Performs a synchronous search as specified by the LDAP URL.
ldap_url_search_st()	Performs a synchronous search with a timeout as specified by the LDAP URL.

The LDAP URL APIs allow the LDAP URL to be preceded by `URL:` and/or enclosed in angle brackets as in

`<URL:ldap://saturn.itso.austin.ibm.com:389/o=Transarc,c=US>`.

LDAP URL searches are associated with an existing LDAP session handle. If the host is not specified in the LDAP URL, the host associated with the existing session handle is assumed. Otherwise a connection is automatically made to the specified host. The search is also affected by session parameters including size and time limits and how aliases and references are handled.

4.5 The Java Naming and Directory Interface (JNDI)

Java is an object-oriented language that is especially suited to the Internet and Web browsers. It allows small applications called applets to be downloaded into a browser over a network and executed in a secure manner, or they execute on the application server itself (then also called servlets). With the proliferation of the World Wide Web, Java has become an important and widespread language. Because LDAP is also becoming an important Internet protocol, it is natural that a Java interface to LDAP would emerge.

An application developer has two choices for accessing LDAP from a Java application. The Java LDAP API, sometimes called JDAP, is an LDAP class library defined in the IETF draft *The Java LDAP Application Program Interface*. For example, Netscape has implemented a Java API Software

Development Kit (SDK) based on this draft. Sun Microsystems has developed the Java Naming and Directory Interface (JNDI) as part of its Java Enterprise API set, which also includes Enterprise Java Beans (EJB) and Java Database Connectivity (JDBC). JNDI is being supported by many vendors including IBM, Hewlett-Packard and Novell.

Both the Java API and JNDI support only a synchronous programming interface. However, a multithreaded Java application can continue processing while one thread blocks on a synchronous LDAP call. The Java API closely follows the LDAP C API while JNDI provides a generalized naming and directory interface. JNDI can access other directory services besides LDAP such as the Network Information System (NIS), Novell Directory Services (NDS), and the Internet Domain Name System (DNS). Because of the wide acceptance of Sun's Java Enterprise API JNDI, is discussed as the Java interface to LDAP.

A naming service organizes and names objects. It provides an association known as a binding between a name and an object. The binding between a name and an object should not be confused with the connection between a client and a server, which is sometimes also called a binding. For example, a file system names and organizes files. The files are the objects that are bound to the names. Given a file name, the file itself can be retrieved.

A directory service can be considered to be a specific type of naming service in which objects bound to names are directory entries. Directory entries are made up of attributes that store values describing the entity represented by the directory entry. The types of directory entries and attributes that can be stored are described by schema.

As discussed above, JNDI provides a generalized naming and directory service interface. For example, JNDI could be used to retrieve files from a file system. In this case, a file system acting as a naming service could return the file that is bound to a particular file name. JNDI could also be used to access an LDAP directory, performing searches and retrieving attributes.

JNDI provides an API that applications use to access a naming and directory service. The naming and directory service could be provided by any of a variety of servers, such as LDAP, NDS, or a file system. JNDI provides a Service Provider Interface (SPI) that enables access to the particular underlying directory service. The SPI is written by the vendor of the underlying naming and directory service and is supplied as a Java class library. This allows arbitrary services providers to be plugged into the JNDI Framework (see Figure 31).

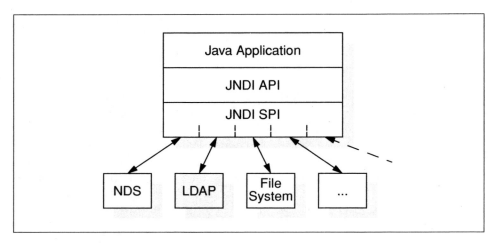

Figure 31. JNDI API and SPI Interfaces

JNDI provides classes that implement a naming interface for applications, such as the file system example, that only look up names and access objects bound to names. JNDI also provides a directory interface that extends the naming interface. The directory interface adds functionality to access attributes and schema.

In JNDI terminology, a name is made up of individual components called *atomic names* that correspond to RDNs in LDAP. A sequence of atomic names is a compound name. An LDAP DN is a compound name. Since the underlying naming and directory services can have different name syntaxes, the SPI provides an implementation of a NameParser that can break a name into its component parts. For example, LDAP RDNs are separated by commas; DNS names are separated by periods, and so on. Composite names are compound names that span different name spaces. For example, an LDAP URL can contain both a DNS and an LDAP name, as, for instance, in `ldap://ldap.mycompany.com/cn=John%20Smith,o=IBM,c=US`.

Names are interpreted within a context. A context can be thought of as a particular node in the Directory Information Tree (DIT). If the current context is `o=IBM,c=US`, then the atomic name `ou=Austin` refers to the child node in the DIT with the DN `ou=Austin,o=IBM,c=US`. The node `ou=Austin,o=IBM,c=US` is also called a subcontext of `o=IBM,c=US`. A name space is traversed from context to subcontext like a file system is traversed from directory to the directory subtree.

The DirContext interface extends the Context interface by adding operations specific to a directory service such as accessing attributes and searching. An application must establish an initial directory context as a starting point from which to do searches or traverse the DIT. The initial directory context is usually the name of an LDAP server.

JNDI provides all of the operations of LDAP Version 3 except for extended operations and controls. Searches use a search filter as defined in *The String Representation of LDAP Search Filters* (RFC 2254). A SearchControls object passed to the search method can be set to control search characteristics such as the scope of the search, the number of entries returned, the time limit, and so on. Also, the entire schema name space can be browsed, and object and attribute schema definitions can be retrieved.

When a directory context is established, it is passed an environment that contains preferences and controls how the directory service is accessed. The environment specifies the SPI to use, security level for binding to the server, and so on. The environment is a Hashtable or Properties list of (key, value) pairs. The environment settings could be coded in the application, retrieved from the System properties, or retrieved from a file. Table 16 lists some of the important environment properties. Different SPIs may support other environment properties and interpret or support values differently.

Table 16. JNDI Directory Context Environment Properties

Environment Property	Use
java.naming.factory.initial	Specifies the SPI
java.naming.provider.url	LDAP URL that specifies the LDAP server
java.naming.ldap.version	Specifies if server supports LDAP Version 2 or 3
java.naming.referral	Specifies if referrals should be followed, ignored, or throw an exception
java.naming.security.authentication	Authentication method used to bind to LDAP server: none, simple, strong
java.naming.security.principal	Identity of user to authenticate
java.naming.security.credentials	Password or other security credential

4.5.1 JNDI Example Program

The following Java program uses JNDI to perform a search and print the attribute values of the directory entries found. It is a simple program that illustrates the basic ideas of:

- Setting up an environment and establishing an initial directory context.

- Setting up a search filter and search controls.
- Stepping through the returned entries and printing the values of the attributes.

```
/*
 * Example JNDI program that performs an LDAP search
 * and parses and prints the results.
 *
 * file: Search.java
 */

import javax.naming.*;
import javax.naming.directory.*;
import java.util.Properties;
import java.util.Enumeration;

class Search  {

public static void main(String[] args) {

  try {
    /* Create an environment for the initial directory context.
       The properties specify the LDAP provider, the LDAP server,
       the LDAP version, and no security (anonymous bind). */

    Properties env = new Properties();
    env.put("java.naming.factory.initial", "com.ibm.jndi.LDAPCtxFactory");
    env.put("java.naming.factory.url.pkgs", "com.ibm.jndi");
    env.put("java.naming.provider.url",
            "ldap://saturn.itso.austin.ibm.com");

    /* Create the initial directory context. */
    DirContext ctx = new InitialDirContext(env);

    /* Set up and perform the search.  Find all people in IBM in the
       United States whose common name starts with Sue or Johan. */
    String base = "o=IBM,c=US";
    String filter = "(|(cn=Sue*)(cn=Johan*))";
    SearchControls constraints = new SearchControls();
    constraints.setSearchScope(SearchControls.SUBTREE_SCOPE);
    NamingEnumeration results = ctx.search(base,filter,constraints);
    /* Print the search results. */
    if (!results.hasMore()) {
      System.out.println("Nothing found.");
    } else {
      /* For each entry found. */
      while (results.hasMore()) {
```

```
        SearchResult sr = (SearchResult) results.next();
        System.out.println(sr.getName());
        Attributes attrs = sr.getAttributes();
        if (attrs == null) {
          System.out.println("No attributes");
        } else {
          /* For each attribute of the entry. */
          for (NamingEnumeration ae = attrs.getAll(); ae.hasMore();) {
            Attribute attr = (Attribute) ae.next();
            String id = attr.getID();
            /* For each value of the attribute. */
            for (Enumeration vals = attr.getAll(); vals.hasMoreElements();
                System.out.println("    "+id + ": " + vals.nextElement()));
          }
        }
      }
    }
  } catch (NamingException e) {
    /* Handle any name/directory exceptions. */
    System.err.println("Search failed: " + e.getMessage());
  } catch (Exception e) {
    /* Handle any other types of exceptions. */
    System.err.println("Non-naming error: " + e.getMessage());
  }
}
}
```

The output of the program executed against a sample directory follows.

```
cn=John Smith, ou=Austin, o=IBM, c=US
    sn: Smith
    title: ISO Deputy, Qual. Tech
    postalcode: 1515
    objectclass: organizationalPerson
    objectclass: person
    objectclass: top
    facsimiletelephonenumber: 1-812-855-5923
    telephonenumber: 1-512-838-6004
    internationalisdnnumber: 755-5923
    cn: John Smith
cn=Sue Kramer, ou=Austin, o=IBM, c=US
    sn: Kramer
    title: ISO Deputy, Qual. Tech
    postalcode: 1515
    objectclass: organizationalPerson
    objectclass: top
    facsimiletelephonenumber: 1-812-855-5923
```

```
internationalisdnnumber: 755-5923
telephonenumber: 1-812-855-5923
cn: Sue Kramer
```

Chapter 5. The Future of LDAP

With LDAP Version 3, a solid foundation for a directory service infrastructure for the Internet was built. As we have seen in previous chapters, most vendor implementations are based on this version or have most features of Version 3 incorporated. But there is still room for enhancements, for example in areas of API support for other program languages, like Java. To define these standards, members of the Internet Engineering Task Force (IETF) work on and submit draft proposals that eventually might become Request for Comments (RFCs). The RFCs describe the idea and the implementation of the major design and technologies for the new functions and features. We describe some important proposed enhancements in the next section.

Although there is not a specific section in this book devoted to it, it should be mentioned that the vendor products will of course be further developed and enhanced, namely in areas such as improved functionality, manageability, and performance. For example, client-side caching could be implemented to improve performance remarkably, especially on multiuser client systems with heavy directory access. Graphical management tools can be added, or existing GUIs may be improved that allow easy configuration and contents management.

As LDAP matures to a de facto standard, it will eventually replace proprietary directory services in vendor products and other standardized middleware solutions, such as the Distributed Computing Environment (DCE). DCE makes heavy use of a directory service and currently uses its own, specific implementation, called Cell Directory Service (CDS). Section 5.2, "Distributed Computing Environment (DCE) and LDAP" on page 133, gives you an introduction on how LDAP will be integrated with DCE. Some other middleware products and their potential use of LDAP are covered in 5.3, "Other Middleware Software" on page 137.

5.1 The IETF LDAP Road Map

The IETF works on several enhancements to LDAP. An LDAP Extension Working Group has been formed within the IETF to define and standardize extensions to LDAP and its use on the Internet. The current state of these enhancements and the working group's plans can be found on the IETF Web site at `www.ietf.org` or in other references listed in Appendix A, "Other LDAP References" on page 139.

Currently, the LDAP Extension Working Group focuses on the following items:

- Authentication

- Access control

- Server-side sorting of search results and paged retrieval of search results

- Language tags

- Dynamic directories

- Referral and knowledge reference maintenance

- LDAP server discovery

- LDAP APIs

- Connectionless LDAP (CLDAP), LDAP over UDP

- Signed directory information

Some of the items above have already been mentioned in 2.1, "Overview of LDAP Architecture" on page 19, as so-called extensions to LDAP Version 3. Since they are extensions, they are not currently included as a standard part of Version 3, but may become part of a future version. Others only exist in early draft versions, and it might be premature to discuss them. The following sections briefly describe some of these topics that appear to be more advanced in the proposal status.

5.1.1 Access Control Requirements for LDAP

There is an Internet Draft titled *Access Control Requirements for LDAP*. This document describes the fundamental requirements for an access control list (ACL) model for the LDAP directory service.

One major requirement for directories, and for information in general, is the ability to securely access, replicate and distribute directory information. Because of the acceptance of LDAP directory services as an access protocol for directory information, there is the need to provide an access control model definition for LDAP directory content among servers within and outside the enterprise. The current version (Version 3) of LDAP does not define an access control model.

The requirements for LDAP access control requirements are divided into multiple areas. These areas cover general security considerations for extensibility, ACL administration and object reuse protection. They also cover semantics and policies, define the way objects can be accessed, how specific policies work and default policies for newly created objects. The last area defines requirements for manageability and usability, such as management of access to resources in an entire subtree.

5.1.2 Scrolling View Browsing of Search Results

With this initiative, the IETF describes a virtual list view control extension for LDAP search operation. It incorporates a "virtual list box" feature that provides support of common scrolling, similar to the window scrolling in many applications. A virtual list can be thought of a graphical user interface that provides a means of better viewing of lists with a large number of entries within a limited size window. This allows lightweight clients to handle large amounts of list data easier because they are handled on the server side.

It allows a client to specify that the server return, for a given LDAP search, only a contiguous subset of the search result. This subset is specified in terms of indices into the ordered list, or in terms of a greater than or equal comparison value.

5.1.3 LDAP Clients Finding LDAP Servers

This initiative discusses the methods available for LDAP clients to discover the existence and locations of LDAP servers. Most of this work is based on previous and ongoing IETF work.

Because LDAP allows to be used to build islands of servers that are not tied together in a single Directory Information Tree (DIT), it might be desirable to have a way how clients can discover LDAP servers.

5.2 Distributed Computing Environment (DCE) and LDAP

DCE is a vendor-neutral, industry-standard distributed computing middleware infrastructure sponsored by the Open Software Foundation (OSF). Although OSF merged with X/Open in 1996 to form The Open Group, DCE is still commonly referred to as OSF DCE. Since this merger, The Open Group has continued to improve and enhance DCE, as evidenced by recent product announcements from various DCE vendors. DCE provides a comprehensive set of tools and services that support reliable, scalable distributed applications in a heterogeneous environment.

DCE provides the following components:

- Threads support for multiple threads of control within a single process, even on operating systems that do not support threads natively.
- Remote Procedure Call (RPC) supports a procedural style programming interface between clients and servers. DCE RPC supports data encryption and is platform-independent by providing data type conversions.

- Security provides authentication, authorization, encryption, and auditing to protect access to data and resources.
- Directory Service provides a central repository for information about resources in the distributed system.
- Distributed Time Service (DTS) keeps the system clocks of distributed computers synchronized.
- Distributed File Service (DFS) provides location transparent access to files stored throughout the network.

It is beyond the scope of this book to explain the details of DCE. More details can be found at www.opengroup.org, or in related Web sites and documentation (see Appendix A, "Other LDAP References" on page 139).

LDAP is being integrated into DCE to take advantage of the common Internet directory infrastructure. This will enable increased sharing of information between DCE and nonDCE environments. Customers will have more choice as to what directory service and administration tools are used to store and manage their DCE directory data.

The DCE Directory Service consists of the Cell Directory Service (CDS), the Global Directory Service (GDS), and the Global Directory Agent (GDA). CDS is a distributed, replicated directory service that stores information about resources in a DCE cell. A DCE cell is a group of machines and resources that are managed as a unit. DCE cells can be as small as a few machines and users or as big as many thousands of machines and tens of thousands of users.

GDS is an X.500-compatible directory that can be used to store information about nonDCE resources. However, many implementations of DCE do not include GDS because it is not widely used.

If applications never access resources outside of their DCE cell, only CDS is required. However, if an application needs to communicate with resources in other DCE cells, the GDA is required. The GDA accesses a global (that is, nonCDS) directory where the names of DCE cells can be registered. This global directory can be either a Domain Name System (DNS) directory or an X.500 directory. The GDA retrieves the address of a CDS server in the remote cell. The remote CDS can then be contacted to find DCE resources in that cell. Using the GDA enables an organization to link multiple DCE cells together using either a private directory on an intranet or a public directory on the Internet.

5.2.1 LDAP Interface for the GDA

One way LDAP is being integrated into DCE is to allow DCE cells to be registered in LDAP directories (see Figure 32). The name of a remote DCE cell and information about the CDS servers in that cell is registered in an LDAP directory server. The GDA in a cell that wants to connect to the remote cell is configured to enable access to the LDAP directory.

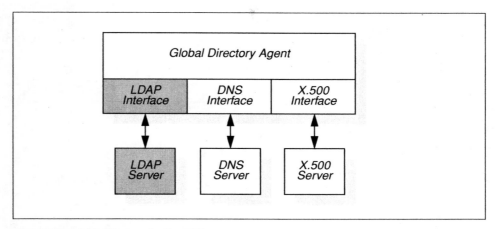

Figure 32. LDAP Interface for the GDA

DCE only supports X.500 and DNS name syntax for cell names. LDAP and X.500 names both follow the same hierarchal naming model, but their syntax is slightly different. X.500 names are written in reverse order and use a slash (/) rather than a comma (,) to separated relative distinguished names. When the GDA is configured to use LDAP, it converts cell names in X.500 format to LDAP format and looks them up in the LDAP directory. If the LDAP directory does not contain the directory entry for the remote cell, the GDA then tries an X.500 server if one is configured.

5.2.2 LDAP Interface for the CDS

DCE provides two programming interfaces to the Directory Service: Name Service Interface (NSI) and the X/Open Directory Service (XDS). XDS is an X.500 compatible interface used to access information in the GDS, and it can also be used to access information in the CDS. However, the use of NSI is much more common in DCE applications.

The NSI API provides functionality that is specifically tailored for use with DCE client and server programs that use RPC. NSI allows servers to register their address and the type of RPC interface they support. This address/interface information is called an RPC binding and is needed by clients that want to contact the server. NSI allows clients to search the CDS for RPC binding information.

NSI was designed to be independent of the directory where the RPC bindings are stored. However, the only supported directory to date has been CDS. NSI will be extended to also support adding and retrieving RPC bindings from an LDAP directory. This will allow servers to advertise their RPC binding information in either CDS or an LDAP directory. Application programs could use either the NSI or the LDAP API when an LDAP directory is used (see Figure 33). An LDAP schema to represent RPC binding information is in the draft stage of development within the IETF.

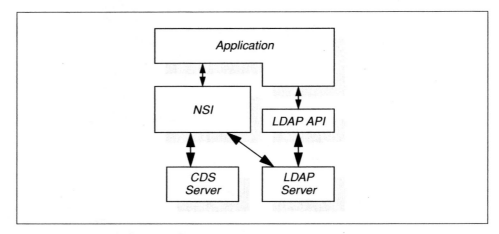

Figure 33. LDAP Interface for NSI

5.2.3 Future LDAP Integration

The LDAP integration projects discussed in 5.2.1, "LDAP Interface for the GDA" on page 135, and 5.2.2, "LDAP Interface for the CDS" on page 135, have been completed by The Open Group and can be expected to appear in vendor DCE offerings. The integration projects discussed below are more speculative, but they are being discussed by The Open Group.

5.2.3.1 Native LDAP Server

CDS was designed as the directory infrastructure for DCE because no other suitable directory was commonly in use in the late 1980s when DCE was being introduced. As LDAP takes on the role of a standard directory infrastructure and DCE components integrate more with LDAP, replacing CDS with LDAP becomes a possibility.

LDAP is currently not as mature as CDS in the areas of replication and access control. As LDAP matures, vendors might begin offering the option of either using CDS or an LDAP service of the customer's choice. Eventually, CDS might not be offered at all.

For easier migration from CDS to LDAP, and for other reasons that might require a parallel operation of CDS and LDAP directories, tools or automated processes may be provided in vendor products that keep these directories in sync.

5.2.3.2 LDAP Interface to Security Registry Data

Information about users, accounts, security policies, and so on is not stored in the CDS, but is stored in a repository controlled by the DCE Security Service. This repository is called the security registry. Although the registry is controlled by the Security Service, it is treated as a part of the CDS name space and accessed with the same administration tools used to access other information in the CDS. As CDS becomes more integrated with or eventually replaced by LDAP, the information in the security registry should also be accessible using LDAP.

Two approaches to providing an LDAP interface to the security registry are being considered. One is to provide an LDAP gateway to the registry or to modify the security server to accept LDAP requests. A second, probably simpler, approach is to eliminate the registry and store the registry information directly in the LDAP-based directory service. As LDAP matures in the areas of access control and security, this second approach becomes more attractive.

5.3 Other Middleware Software

As we will see in Appendix B, "LDAP Products and Services" on page 143, most vendors of any kind of directory server or directory-enabled client products have (or will shortly) implemented some kind of LDAP support, either as an interface to access their directory information or as a client to access external LDAP directories.

Besides directory server and directory-enabled client products, there is an important family of application-enabling products, also called middleware software. The Distributed Computing Environment (DCE), as mentioned in the last sections, is only one of these enablers. Others might be databases, network operating systems (in a broader context), and distributed object brokers. They all share a common problem: They all need to have some sort of directory to store location and service information. Since they are distributed services, a repository must be in place that can be searched for, such as the name and location of a remote service.

This is exactly where LDAP comes into play as a standardized method as opposed to proprietary directories.

Although not formally announced or committed in any form at the time this book was written, there is certainly some good speculation around that such middleware products may exploit LDAP in future releases.

5.4 The Directory-Enabled Networks Initiative

In September 1997, Cisco Systems Inc. and Microsoft Corp. announced the so-called Directory-Enabled Networks Initiative (DEN) as a result of a collaborative work. Many companies, such as IBM, either support this initiative or even actively participate in ad hoc working groups (ADWGs). DEN represents an information model specification for an integrated directory that stores information about people, network devices and applications. The DEN schema defines the object classes and their related attributes for those objects. In such, DEN is a key piece to building intelligent networks, where products from multiple vendors can store and retrieve topology and configuration related data. Since DEN is a relatively new specification, products supporting it cannot be expected until about one to two years after its first draft was published late in 1997.

Of special interest is that the DEN specification defines LDAP Version 3 as the core protocol for accessing DEN information, which makes information available to LDAP-enabled clients and/or network devices.

More information about the DEN initiative can be found on the founders' Web sites or at `www.universe.digex.net/~murchiso/den/`.

Appendix A. Other LDAP References

As mentioned throughout the book, this appendix lists references to other sources of information about LDAP. Where suitable, some background information is provided as well.

Please note that, due to the dynamic character of the Internet, some URLs to particular Web sites may already have become invalid by the time you read this book.

A.1 The Internet Engineering Task Force (IETF)

The Internet Engineering Task Force (IETF) is an open international community to design and discuss future Internet technologies. The people belonging to this group are network designers, operators, and researchers from commercial and non-commercial organizations. The task is to design open standards for common use in the Internet. The group is open to any interested individual.

The actual work of the IETF is done in workgroups, which are organized by topics into several areas, for example routing, transport, security, and so on. The workgroups are grouped into areas and managed by area directors. These area directors are members of the Internet Engineering Steering Group (IESG). Providing architectural oversight is the Internet Architecture Board (IAB). Both the IESG and IAB are chartered by the Internet Society (ISOC) for these purposes. The general area director also serves as the chair of IETF and IESG and is an ex-official member of the IAB.

The central coordinator is the Internet Assigned Numbers Authority (IANA), which coordinates the unique assignment of parameter values for Internet protocols. The IANA is chartered by the ISOC to act as the clearinghouse to assign and coordinate the use of numerous Internet protocol parameters.

New technologies are invented and discussed in so-called IETF drafts (or Internet Drafts). These drafts and the basic design ideas are posted to the mailing list and are discussed until general consensus is reached to stop work on the draft or progress it to RFC by requesting approval of the area director and the IESG. At approval, an RFC number is assigned. The RFC is the base description for new versions and enhancements.

The IETF Web site can be reached at:

```
http://www.ietf.org/
```

On this Web site, there are links to IETF Workgroups, Internet Drafts, mailing lists, and so on.

A.2 The University of Michigan (UMICH)

The University of Michigan was and still is an important contributor in the development of LDAP and can be considered a reliable, neutral source for extensive information and program source code for LDAP servers and clients.

The UMICH's home page is at:

```
http://www.umich.edu/
```

The UMICH's LDAP page can be accessed at:

```
http://www.umich.edu/~dirsvcs/ldap/
```

This latter page contains, among others, links to online LDAP documentation from the UMICH and others and downloadable software, most of which as source code.

A.3 Software Development Kits

Below, you find some URLs where you can download SDKs offered by different vendors for a wide variety of platforms. You might find some useful information, such as documentation and FAQ (Frequently Asked Questions) lists and links to other interesting LDAP-related places there as well.

The University of Michigan's LDAP server code, a C language SDK, and other links to documentation and LDAP mailing lists can be found at the following link:

```
http://www.umich.edu/~dirsvcs/ldap/
```

IBM's C and Java SDKs can be found at:

```
http://www.networking.ibm.com/ldap/ldaphome.html
```

Netscape offers a C and a Java SDKs at:

```
http://developer.netscape.com/software/sdks/index.html
```

A.4 Other Sources

Below is a list of Web links sorted upon common criteria.

A.4.1 Vendors Mentioned in this Book

The following links point you the home pages of the vendors that have been mentioned throughout the book.

IBM — `http://www.ibm.com/`

Tivoli — `http://www.tivoli.com/`

Lotus — `http://www.lotus/com/`

Netscape — `http://www.netscape.com/`

Critical Angle — `http://www.critical-angle.com/`

Novell — `http://www.novell.com/`

Microsoft — `http://www.microsoft.com/`

A.4.2 LDAP, General

For general information about LDAP, please refer to the Web sites of the IETF and the University of Michigan as listed earlier in this appendix. If you search the Web for 'LDAP', there will be thousands of hits. Following are just a few links to related Web sites that you might find interesting.

An LDAP Roadmap & FAQs:

```
http://www.kingsmountain.com/ldapRoadmap.shtml
http://www.critical-angle.com/ldapworld/ldapfaq.html
```

IBM LDAP client Web page:

```
http://www.networking.ibm.com/ldap/ldaphome.html
```

IBM eNetwork Security and Directory library:

```
http://www.software.ibm.com/ts/dsseries/library/
```

Critical Angle Inc. (Innosoft International Inc.) hosts a series of interesting information and links at:

```
http://www.critical-angle.com/ldapworld/index.html
```

A System Administrator's view of LDAP:

```
http://people.netscape.com/bjm/whyLDAP.html
```

A collection of information related to DEN (Directory-Enabled Networks):

```
http://www.universe.digex.net/~murchiso/den/
```

Directory Deployment and Installation (Netscape):

```
http://home.netscape.com/eng/server/directory/3.0/deploy/contents.html
```

A.4.3 Request for Comments (RFCs)

A good source for accessing RFCs with search capabilities is provided by the Information Sciences Institute (ISI) at:

```
http://www.isi.edu/rfc-editor/rfc.html
```

This ISI Web site includes a number of links to other RFC sources. If, for some reason, you cannot access the link above, try one of the following:

```
http://www.pasteur.fr/other/computer/RFC/
http://www.garlic.com/~lynn/rfcietf.html
http://www.nexor.com/public/rfc/index/rfc.html
http://www.csl.sony.co.jp/rfc/
```

A.4.4 Security

The SSL Protocol Version 3.0:

```
http://home.netscape.com/eng/ssl3/ssl-toc.html
```

Simple Authentication and Security Layer (SASL), RFC 2222:

```
ftp://ftp.isi.edu/in-notes/rfc2222.txt
```

SASL Mechanisms:

```
ftp://ftp.isi.edu/in-notes/iana/assignments/sasl-mechanisms
```

SASL Service Names:

```
ftp://ftp.isi.edu/in-notes/iana/assignments/gssapi-service-names
```

The TLS Protocol, Version 1.0 (Internet Draft):

```
http://www.ietf.org/internet-drafts/draft-ietf-tls-protocol-05.txt
```

Appendix B. LDAP Products and Services

Many LDAP-compatible products are already available on the market. They either exploit LDAP directly or enable other applications to use LDAP. More will become available as LDAP evolves. This appendix presents a brief overview of some products from IBM and other vendors that are worth mentioning. The list of products surveyed here is not intended to be exhaustive, but covers some widespread and influential products. At the time of writing, there were well over 50 products available on the market that are either LDAP servers, LDAP-to-X.500 gateways or other applications that exploit LDAP in some way. We cannot list and explain them all because such a list would become outdated in a short while.

In addition to private LDAP directories maintained on various private intranets, publicly accessible LDAP directories are also available. Some of the major publicly accessible LDAP directories are also surveyed. Like the product survey, the public directory survey cannot be complete and may not be up to date by the time you read this. You should always refer to the respective vendor or browse their Web sites to have the most current information on products and features.

B.1 IBM Product Offerings

IBM strongly supports the LDAP standard and actively contributes to the work being done in the related IETF working groups. As a result, IBM offers a series of products and will introduce more that support the LDAP standard. The following is a description of these offerings; for more details, please study the official product announcement documentation.

B.1.1 IBM eNetwork LDAP Directory

IBM eNetwork LDAP Directory is based on IETF LDAP Version 2 (RFC 1777) plus some extensions for LDAP Version 3. The implementations on AIX and OS/390 utilize IBM's DB2 relational database as the directory data storage facility. A DB2 single-user component is included with the eNetwork LDAP Directory on AIX. IBM eNetwork LDAP Directory standards are based on:

- RFC 1777 – Lightweight Directory Access Protocol
- RFC 1778 – String Representation of Standard Attribute Syntaxes
- RFC 1779 – String Representation of Distinguished Names
- RFC 1823 – LDAP Application Program Interface
- RFC 1960 – A String Representation of LDAP Search Filters

IBM eNetwork LDAP Directory provides Secure Sockets Layer (SSL) Version 3 support, both for the directory server and client. SSL provides encryption of data and authentication using X.509v3 pubic-key certificates. The directory may be configured to run with or without SSL support. IBM eNetwork LDAP Directory also supports LDAP referrals, allowing directory operations to be redirected to another LDAP directory server. Replication of the LDAP directory is supported, which allows for additional copies of the directory to be available for directory read operations, thus increasing performance and reliability of access to the directory information.

IBM eNetwork LDAP Directory ships with AIX and is included in the Security Server for OS/390. IBM plans to make eNetwork LDAP Directory available on OS/400, Windows NT, and Solaris later in 1998. At the same time, work is on the way to support the full LDAP Version 3 level.

B.1.2 IBM eNetwork X.500 Directory for AIX

IBM eNetwork X.500 Directory for AIX, Version 1.0, (X.500 Directory) is an advanced electronic directory product that provides a robust, high-performance and a highly scalable implementation. Secure Socket Layer (SSL) technology, used with Lightweight Directory Access Protocol (LDAP) and Hypertext Transfer Protocol (HTTP), is incorporated into the directory server. The main components are:

- X.500 Directory Server: Optimized for demanding, high-end applications requiring a very large capacity X.500 or LDAP directory service and very high search rates in hierarchically structured data.

- Desktop Directory User Agents (DUAs) for Windows and Macintosh: Stand-alone DUAs that provide a fully graphical interface for accessing the directory.

- Web-based DUA and Web Administrative Facilities: Provide directory access and directory administration over the World Wide Web.

- LDAP Application Development Package (ADP): Provides elements required and supports the AIX, Windows NT, Windows 95, Solaris, and HP-UX platforms. Also included is support for the Java Naming and Directory Interface (JNDI), which provides for the development of Java applications that need to access an LDAP directory server.

Because of U.S. export regulations, multiple versions are available that support different levels of encryption for U.S. domestic and international use.

B.1.3 IBM eNetwork LDAP Client Pack for Multiplatforms

The IBM eNetwork LDAP Client Pack for Multiplatforms provides elements required to develop LDAP client applications that access LDAP directory servers (LDAP Version 2 and 3) and supports the IBM AIX, Windows NT and 95, Solaris, and HP-UX platforms. It also includes support for the Java Naming and Directory Interface (JNDI), which provides for the development of Java applications that need to access and LDAP directory service.

The predecessor, the IBM LDAP Client Pack for Multiplatforms, has been announced and has been available from IBM since mid-1997. It was updated with new technology in early 1998 to include support for LDAP Version 3 and Java. The LDAP Client Pack consists of an LDAP shared library, C header files, sample programs, and online documentation in HTML. The LDAP API, based on RFC 1823 and extensions in the University of Michigan LDAP 3.3 distribution, provides:

- Typical directory functions such as read, write and search
- Client authentication to the directory service using either no authentication or simple (password) authentication
- Powerful, yet relatively simple to use set of interface commands
- Synchronous or asynchronous interface access
- Client/Server model using TCP/IP connections from client to server

The IBM LDAP Client Pack supports the following standards:

- RFC 1777 – Lightweight Directory Access Protocol
- RFC 1778 – String Representation of Standard Attribute Syntaxes
- RFC 1779 – String Representation of Distinguished Names (DNs)
- RFC 1823 – LDAP Application Program Interface
- RFC 2251 – Lightweight Directory Access Protocol
- RFC 2252 – LDAP V3 Attribute Syntax Definitions
- RFC 2253 – UTF-8 String Representation of DNs
- RFC 2254 – The String Representation of LDAP Search Filters
- RFC 2255 – The LDAP URL Format

Different versions of the LDAP Client Pack are available. They differ in the encryption module (40-, 56-, or 128-bit SSL), which is subject to United States export regulations.

IBM eNetwork LDAP Client Pack for Multiplatforms is included in IBM eNetwork X.500 Directory for AIX (see B.1.2, "IBM eNetwork X.500 Directory for AIX" on page 144) and will be included in an upcoming Bonus Pack for

AIX. It is also available separately as a Program Request for Price Quotation (PRPQ), which means it is available only by direct request.

B.2 Lotus Domino

Lotus Development Corp. concentrates on platform-independent desktop and groupware solutions. Lotus Domino, the latest groupware server product, incorporates not only a framework for individual application development but also includes all standard functions for a collaborative working environment in small and large organizations, such as e-mail, shared distributed databases, and easy desktop integration. Lotus Domino Server and the Lotus Notes clients are available for all major platforms.

As a key function for most of its underlying services, Domino includes an extensive address book (the Domino Directory Notes Address Book, NAB) that stores people information and system-related data. Multiple Domino servers work together and share their address book information, allowing an organization to easily scale up.

Beginning with its Release 4.6, Lotus Domino also incorporates an LDAP service that allows LDAP clients to access the information stored in the address book. With Domino R4.6 support for LDAP, other LDAP-compliant applications, whether inside or outside the enterprise, can locate resources in a Domino directory. Non-Notes clients that are LDAP-compliant can interact with the Domino Directory Notes Address Book (NAB). A Domino server can also act as a gateway to other LDAP servers, for example a public Four11 service.

Domino R4.6 supports LDAP Version 2 and attributes defined by the Lightweight Internet Person Schema (LIPS), a related standard. While full search capability is provided, update operations are not supported. Native LDAP support enables users of POP3, IMAP or other Internet mail clients that support LDAP to perform name lookups in the Domino directory when addressing e-mails. Domino Server administrators can set up their Domino Servers to perform LDAP lookups into LDAP-compliant public directories on the Internet. The LDAP service in Domino 4.6 also supports SSL, storage of X.509v3 certificates, and referrals.

Starting with Domino 5.0, the full LDAP Version 3 standard will be supported. Add and modify operations to the NAB will be supported as well.

B.3 Tivoli User Administration: LDAP Endpoint

Tivoli Management Architecture is a highly sophisticated, universal systems management framework available for all major platforms, including Windows NT/95 and many UNIX brands.

Tivoli User Administration is a management application that runs on top of the Tivoli framework. Briefly speaking, it consists of an extensive database and a number of endpoint adapters. The core database, together with a graphical management user interface, allows to manage user accounts independent of any underlying system. The database supports a large number of attributes suitable for almost any kind of target environment. The adapters then interface this database with any underlying operating system or application. For example, a UNIX adapter propagates (distributes) the relevant attributes from the user administration database to the relevant database (files) on the destination UNIX system(s). The reverse process, called population, is supported, too. Population collects the actual user configuration data from a destination environment and stores it in the database for subsequent management. Figure 34 depicts this relationship.

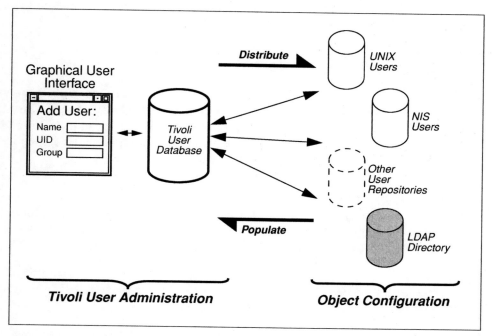

Figure 34. Tivoli Database Versus the Real Configuration

Through the addition of an LDAP adapter (also called an *Endpoint* in Tivoli terminology), Tivoli User Administration is enriched in its functionality to manage LDAP directory data (while other system-related management and monitoring can be done using other Tivoli systems management and monitoring functionality). This adapter runs on any managed node which may or may not be the on same system as the Tivoli Administration Server, also called the TMR Server (Tivoli Management Region) Server. Since LDAP is a system-independent standard, the actual LDAP service can be run on any platform. This approach centers the Tivoli User Administration database and all other user data repositories, including the LDAP directory, are kept in sync with the master Tivoli database. An administrator only uses one common user interface and one single tool to manage user accounts, no matter whether the actual users exist on a UNIX system, in an NIS domain, in LDAP, or in any other of the many supported endpoints.

It should be mentioned that the Tivoli User Administration also supports a command line interface for all operations. This allows automation of administration tasks from within command language programs.

At the time this book was written, the LDAP Endpoint was still under development and final testing. The product was supposed to be available shortly thereafter.

B.4 Other LDAP Server Products

There are over 30 native LDAP server or LDAP-to-X.500 gateway products available on the market (spring 1998). We briefly describe three products that are well known in the following sections. For the latest information, or if you need more details, we refer you directly to the vendors; their URLs are provided below for your convenience.

B.4.1 Netscape Directory Server

Netscape's Directory Server, as part of their Suite Spot product suite, combines the directory services for the various Internet services. Directory Server is a native LDAP implementation that supports LDAP Version 2 and Version 3 operations. Some of the features are:

- Supports referrals
- Uses either a native database or an external RDBMS
- Includes a tool that synchronizes Windows NT domain-based directories, (NT 3.51 and 4.0) including user, group and password information
- Supports flexible replication

- Stores ACLs with each entry for access security

Directory Server is available for all major UNIX platforms and Windows NT. It comes with an SKD that allows a programmer to build directory-enabled applications.

For more information, please browse the relevant pages at www.netscape.com.

B.4.2 Novell LDAP Services for NDS

Novell Directory Services (NDS) is the directory service that comes with Novell's NetWare network operating system (NOS). It has long been on the market and provides advanced directory services, some of which are not available in current LDAP services. With the addition of LDAP Services for NDS (which is otherwise a proprietary directory), Novell opened NDS in a way such that LDAP clients can access information stored in NDS. This was done in response to the fact that LDAP is emerging to a de facto standard for directory access.

For more information, Novell's Web site is www.novell.com.

B.4.3 Microsoft Active Directory

Active Directory is Microsoft's proprietary implementation of a directory service that runs on Windows NT Server 5.0 (and may be supported on other products from Microsoft as well). It replaces the NT domain database of earlier NT versions and overcomes some of its limitations. The domain concept with a single domain database was introduced over 10 years ago and has limitations in large installations because of scalability and manageability shortcomings. Active Directory, however, is not an all-new technology and still carries the concept of domains with it. It introduces, for example, a new data storage engine that allows extensible objects and promises better scalability, but it can only be replicated as a whole. This means that an Active Directory directory cannot be partitioned into smaller pieces for easy replication or management.

While Active Directory may have some attractive functions specific to those bound to the NT domain concept, it lacks some others. Active Directory is supported on the Windows NT platform only and because of its proprietary nature, it cannot easily be substituted with other products.

Active Directory is not an LDAP directory, nor is LDAP meant to be the primary access protocol or API. It is mentioned here because, obviously due to the importance of LDAP in an open computing environment, an LDAP interface was added to it, allowing clients using LDAP operations to access data stored in the directory. Additionally, an Active Directory server can access other servers that are using LDAP.

Microsoft's Web site has more information at `www.microsoft.com`.

B.5 LDAP Enabled Clients and Applications

It is beyond the scope of this book to compile a complete list of vendor applications that exploit LDAP directory services. Instead, we refer you back to 1.6, "The Quick Start: A Public LDAP Example" on page 16, where a simple example shows how an LDAP directory can be used. As mentioned there, Web browsers are perfect examples of applications that benefit most from an LDAP service. Since most Web browsers also include a mail client, users can look up e-mail addresses of the recipients directly through the mail client search tool, no matter whether the directory is the local, personal directory or a remote LDAP directory.

Another area that is likely to embrace an LDAP directory service is networking equipment. Network administrators and routers can store and retrieve network-related information from a single point, allowing a network administrator to manage a network much more efficiently as compared to when he or she has to maintain many different configuration databases in individual devices. This is the basic idea behind the Directory-Enabled Networks initiative (DEN) described in 5.4, "The Directory-Enabled Networks Initiative" on page 138.

B.6 LDAP Development Kits and Tools

Most vendors that offer LDAP products also offer SDKs, either together with the products or as separate kits, for directory-enabled application development. For URL addresses to the SDK downloads, we refer you to A.3, "Software Development Kits" on page 140.

A good source for a vendor-neutral kit is the University of Michigan (UMICH). As a major contributor to the LDAP standard and development, UMICH has development kits for LDAP servers and clients available on their Web site, along with valuable documentation.

Besides UMICH's software development kit, there are SDKs available from IBM, Netscape, and others.

B.7 Public LDAP Services

As we have seen in the introductory example in 1.6, "The Quick Start: A Public LDAP Example" on page 16, there are already a number of public providers that offer LDAP directory services on the Internet. Below is a short list, conducted from research on the Internet, of such public LDAP directory service providers. Please bear in mind that the list cannot be complete and might even contain outdated references at the time you read this book. The selections provided do not imply any recommendation or rating. Given is the host name of the server machine that provides this service; they all listen on the default LDAP port 389. For additional information, such as corporate profiles and additional services, please refer to their home pages (URL provided in parenthesis):

Four11 — `ldap.four11.com` (`www.four11.com`)

InfoSpace — `ldap.infospace.com` (`www.infospace.com`)

WhoWhere — `ldap.whowhere.com` (`www.whowhere.com`)

Bigfoot — `ldap.bigfoot.com` (`www.bigfoot.com`)

Switchboard — `ldap.switchboard.com` (`www.switchboard.com`)

Delivery of Advanced Network Technology to Europe (DANTE) is a service that connects universities and research laboratories in Europe. They offer a Web-to-X.500 gateway to selected X.500 Directories in the research and university community at:

```
www.dante.net:8888/M
```

DANTE also has an extensive list of other general directory and LDAP directory services available at:

```
www.dante.net/np/pdi.html
```

Reminder: LDAP Uses Port 389!

As a reminder (we mentioned this in chapter 1), your browser might not be able to connect to any of the services listed above if your browser is connected to a private network, connected to the Internet through a firewall. This is because most firewalls and administrators are not aware of LDAP traffic on port 389, which is therefore blocked out. If this is the case, you should talk to your firewall administrator.

Alternatively, your company might already have internal LDAP servers that you were not aware of. Ask your system administrator while arguing with him or her about the LDAP port on the firewall!

Appendix C. LDAP C Language API Functions and Error Codes

As a complement to Chapter 4, "Building LDAP-Enabled Applications" on page 85, this appendix lists all LDAP API function calls and error codes for LDAP Version 3. A short description is provided with the function calls.

> **Note**
>
> The information given in this appendix is based on an Internet Draft and is provided for your convenience only to complement the programming samples explained in Chapter 4, "Building LDAP-Enabled Applications" on page 85. For the most accurate and current information, you should always consult the latest documentation provided in the Internet Draft or RFC, or refer to the documentation that came with your product(s).

C.1 C Language API Calls

Some of the functions listed in the following tables may have been mentioned earlier in Chapter 4, "Building LDAP-Enabled Applications" on page 85. As mentioned in that chapter, a trailing "_s" in the function's name indicates that the function operates in synchronous mode.

C.1.1 Functions to Establish and Terminate a Connection

The functions listed here in Table 17 are used to initialize a connection and authenticate a client to an LDAP server. They are usually invoked at the very beginning of the conversation with the LDAP server, with one exception: The `ldap_unbind()` is used to close the connection to the LDAP server.

Table 17. Functions that Initialize and Terminate a Connection

Function	Description
ldap_init(), ldap_open()	Initialize a session with an LDAP server.
ldap_simple_bind(), ldap_simple_bind_s()	Initiate a simple bind to an LDAP server.
ldap_sasl_bind(), ldap_sasl_bind_s()	Authenticate the client to an LDAP server using the Simple Authentication Security Layer.
ldap_set_rebind_proc()	Reauthenticate, for example when another server through a referral result message is involved.

Function	Description
ldap_unbind()	Close an LDAP session, dispose the session handle.

C.1.2 Session-Handling Functions

These functions (Table 18) are closely related to the previously mentioned functions. They are used to influence the session handle options once a connection is initialized.

Table 18. Session-Handling Functions

Function	Description
ldap_set_option()	Set the value of a specified option.
ldap_get_option()	Get the value of a specified option.

C.1.3 Interacting with the Server

The functions listed here in Table 19 send and receive data through the network to/from an LDAP server.

Table 19. Functions that Send or Receive Data

Function	Description
ldap_search(), ldap_search_s()	Initiates a synchronous or asynchronous search of an LDAP directory.
ldap_search_ext(), ldap_search_ext_s()	Like ldap_search() but server and client controls can get specified.
ldap_search_st()	Like ldap_search_s(), but a time value for the API to wait until the results are received can get specified.
ldap_compare(), ldap_compare_s()	Compares a given attribute value against the actual one stored within the LDAP server.
ldap_compare_ext(), ldap_compare_ext_s()	Like ldap_compare but the comparison of binary values is possible. LDAP V3 server and client controls are supported.
ldap_modify(), ldap_modify_s()	Adds, deletes or replaces values of an attribute.
ldap_modify_ext(), ldap_modify_ext_s()	Like ldap_modify() but LDAP V3 server and client controls are supported.

Function	Description
`ldap_modrdn2()`, `ldap_modrdn2_s()`	Changes the name (RDN) of an entry.
`ldap_rename()`, `ldap_rename_s()`	Modifies the distinguished name of an entry.
`ldap_add()`, `ldap_add_s()`	Add an entry to an LDAP directory.
`ldap_add_ext()`, `ldap_add_ext_s()`	Like `ldap_add()`, LDAP V3 client and server controls are supported.
`ldap_delete()`, `ldap_delete_s()`	Deletion of leaf entries
`ldap_delete_ext()`, `ldap_delete_ext_s()`	Like `ldap_delete()`, LDAP V3 client and server controls are supported.
`ldap_extended_operation()`, `ldap_extended_operation_s()`	Sending of extended LDAP operations, used as general protocol extensibility mechanism.
`ldap_abandon()`, `ldap_abandon_ext()`	Abandon operation in progress. LDAP V3 client and server control supported by `ldap_abandon_ext()`.
`ldap_result()`	Obtaining the result of a previously issued asynchronous operation.

C.1.4 Error Handling

The functions for error handling, those used to retrieve the errors of previous LDAP function calls, are listed in Table 20.

Table 20. Functions for Error Handling

Function	Description
`ldap_parse_result()`	Returns error code of previous API function call.
`ldap_parse_sasl_bind()`	Returns error code of a SASL bind call.
`ldap_parse_extended_result()`	Returns error code of previous extended operation.
`ldap_result2error()`	Converts numeric error code in error string.

C.1.5 Analyzing Results

The following functions (Table 21) are used to step through the results obtained by synchronous or asynchronous search functions.

Table 21. Parsing the Results

Function	Description
`ldap_count_messages()`	Counts number of messages in the LDAP message structure.
`ldap_first_message()`	Returns first message in a chain of results obtained by `ldap_result()`.
`ldap_next_message()`	Returns entry in a chain of results obtained by `ldap_result()`.
`ldap_first_entry()`	Returns first entry in a chain of search results.
`ldap_next_entry()`	Returns next entry in a chain of search results.
`ldap_count_entries()`	Counts the number of entries returned by a search operation.
`ldap_first_reference()`, `ldap_next_reference()`	Retrieving and stepping through a list of continuation references obtained by a search result.
`ldap_parse_reference()`	Extracts referrals and controls from a search result.
`ldap_first_attribute()`, `ldap_next_attribute()`	Stepping through a list of attributes returned with an entry.
`ldap_get_values()`	Get values of a given nonbinary attribute.
`ldap_get_values_len()`	Get values of a given attribute.
`ldap_count_values()`, `ldap_count_values_len()`	Count returned values of a attribute.
`ldap_get_dn()`	Retrieve the name of an entry.
`ldap_explode_dn()`, `ldap_explode_rdn()`	Breaks up a DN or RDN in its components.
`ldap_dn2ufn()`	Converts DN to a user-friendly format using RFC 1781, Using the OSI Directory to Achieve User Friendly Naming.
`ldap_get_entry_controls()`	Extracts LDAP controls from an entry.

C.1.6 Freeing Memory

The functions listed in Table 22 are used to free memory occupied by search results, attribute values, and so on.

Table 22. Memory-Freeing Functions

Function	Description
`ldap_ber_free()`	Frees a buffer used by `ldap_first_attribute()` and `ldap_next_attribute()` to keep track of the current position in an entry.
`ldap_msgfree()`	Frees results of previous call to `ldap_result` or an synchronous search routine.
`ldap_memfree()`	Frees memory occupied by LDAP library functions such as `ldap_next_attributes()` or `ldap_get_dn()`.
`ldap_value_free()`	Frees memory occupied by values returned through `ldap_get_values()` or `ldap_get_values_len()`.

C.1.7 Other Functions

The functions listed here in Table 23 carry out various other operations that are not covered by any other cathegory above.

Table 23. Other Functions

Function	Description
`ldap_msgtype()`	Returns the type of an LDAP message.
`ldap_msgid()`	Returns the ID of an LDAP message passed as a parameter to an asynchronous call.
`ldap_version()`	Retrieves basic information about the API implementation, such as SDK version or protocol version.
`ldap_control_free()`, `ldap_controls_free()`	Disposes a single client control or an array of client controls allocated by LDAP API calls.

C.2 LDAP API Error Codes

Listed below are the error codes as returned by many of the LDAP C API functions. Some of them indicate local errors; some are set in the session handle structure by the LDAP server. All error codes correspond to positive integer (hexadecimal values are given in parentheses after the constant) defined in the header file of your SDK.

```
LDAP_SUCCESS (0x00)
LDAP_OPERATIONS_ERROR (0x01)
LDAP_PROTOCOL_ERROR (0x02)
LDAP_TIMELIMIT_EXCEEDED (0x03)
LDAP_SIZELIMIT_EXCEEDED (0x04)
LDAP_COMPARE_FALSE (0x05)
LDAP_COMPARE_TRUE (0x06)
LDAP_STRONG_AUTH_NOT_SUPPORTED (0x07)
LDAP_STRONG_AUTH_REQUIRED (0x08)
LDAP_REFERRAL (0x0a)                            -- new in LDAPv3
LDAP_ADMINLIMIT_EXCEEDED (0x0b)                 -- new in LDAPv3
LDAP_UNAVAILABLE_CRITICAL_EXTENSION (0x0c)      -- new in LDAPv3
LDAP_CONFIDENTIALITY_REQUIRED (0x0d)            -- new in LDAPv3
LDAP_SASL_BIND_IN_PROGRESS (0x0e)               -- new in LDAPv3
LDAP_NO_SUCH_ATTRIBUTE (0x10)
LDAP_UNDEFINED_TYPE (0x11)
LDAP_INAPPROPRIATE_MATCHING (0x12)
LDAP_CONSTRAINT_VIOLATION (0x13)
LDAP_TYPE_OR_VALUE_EXISTS (0x14)
LDAP_INVALID_SYNTAX (0x15)
LDAP_NO_SUCH_OBJECT (0x20)
LDAP_ALIAS_PROBLEM (0x21)
LDAP_INVALID_DN_SYNTAX (0x22)
LDAP_IS_LEAF (0x23)                             -- not used in LDAPv3
LDAP_ALIAS_DEREF_PROBLEM (0x24)
LDAP_INAPPROPRIATE_AUTH (0x30)
LDAP_INVALID_CREDENTIALS (0x31)
LDAP_INSUFFICIENT_ACCESS (0x32)
LDAP_BUSY (0x33)
LDAP_UNAVAILABLE (0x34)
LDAP_UNWILLING_TO_PERFORM (0x35)
DAP_LOOP_DETECT (0x36)
LDAP_NAMING_VIOLATION (0x40)
LDAP_OBJECT_CLASS_VIOLATION (0x41)
LDAP_NOT_ALLOWED_ON_NONLEAF (0x42)
LDAP_NOT_ALLOWED_ON_RDN (0x43)
LDAP_ALREADY_EXISTS (0x44)
LDAP_NO_OBJECT_CLASS_MODS (0x45)
LDAP_RESULTS_TOO_LARGE (0x46)                   -- reserved for CLDAP
```

```
LDAP_AFFECTS_MULTIPLE_DSAS (0x47)                    -- new in LDAPv3
LDAP_OTHER (0x50)
LDAP_SERVER_DOWN (0x51)
LDAP_LOCAL_ERROR (0x52)
LDAP_ENCODING_ERROR (0x53)
LDAP_DECODING_ERROR (0x54)
LDAP_TIMEOUT (0x55)
LDAP_AUTH_UNKNOWN (0x56)
LDAP_FILTER_ERROR (0x57)
LDAP_USER_CANCELLED (0x58)
LDAP_PARAM_ERROR (0x59)
LDAP_NO_MEMORY (0x5a)
LDAP_CONNECT_ERROR (0x5b)
LDAP_NOT_SUPPORTED (0x5c)
LDAP_CONTROL_NOT_FOUND (0x5d)
LDAP_NO_RESULTS_RETURNED (0x5e)
LDAP_MORE_RESULTS_TO_RETURN (0x5f)
LDAP_CLIENT_LOOP (0x60)
LDAP_REFERRAL_LIMIT_EXCEEDED (0x61)
```

Appendix D. Special Notices

This publication is intended to help network and infrastructure professionals understand the concepts and basics of LDAP. The information in this publication is not intended as the specification of any programming interfaces that are provided by any product from either IBM nor any other vendor. See the PUBLICATIONS section of the IBM Programming Announcements of related products for more information about what publications are considered to be product documentation.

References in this publication to IBM products, programs or services do not imply that IBM intends to make these available in all countries in which IBM operates. Any reference to an IBM product, program, or service is not intended to state or imply that only IBM's product, program, or service may be used. Any functionally equivalent program that does not infringe any of IBM's intellectual property rights may be used instead of the IBM product, program or service.

Information in this book was developed in conjunction with use of the equipment specified, and is limited in application to those specific hardware and software products and levels.

IBM may have patents or pending patent applications covering subject matter in this document. The furnishing of this document does not give you any license to these patents. You can send license inquiries, in writing, to the IBM Director of Licensing, IBM Corporation, 500 Columbus Avenue, Thornwood, NY 10594 USA.

Licensees of this program who wish to have information about it for the purpose of enabling: (i) the exchange of information between independently created programs and other programs (including this one) and (ii) the mutual use of the information which has been exchanged, should contact IBM Corporation, Dept. 600A, Mail Drop 1329, Somers, NY 10589 USA.

Such information may be available, subject to appropriate terms and conditions, including in some cases, payment of a fee.

The information contained in this document has not been submitted to any formal IBM test and is distributed AS IS. The information about non-IBM ("vendor") products in this manual has been supplied by the vendor and IBM assumes no responsibility for its accuracy or completeness. The use of this information or the implementation of any of these techniques is a customer responsibility and depends on the customer's ability to evaluate and integrate them into the customer's operational environment. While each item may have been reviewed by IBM for accuracy in a specific situation, there is no guarantee that the same or similar results will be obtained elsewhere. Customers attempting to adapt these techniques to their own environments do so at their own risk.

The following document contains examples of data and reports used in daily business operations. To illustrate them as completely as possible, the examples contain the names of individuals, companies, brands, and products. All of these names are fictitious and any similarity to the names and addresses used by an actual business enterprise is entirely coincidental.

The following terms are trademarks of the International Business Machines Corporation in the United States and/or other countries:

AIX ®	eNetwork
IBM ®	RS/6000 ®
OS/390 ®	OS/400 ®
OS/2 ®	DB2 ®

The following terms are trademarks of other companies:

Java and HotJava are trademarks of Sun Microsystems, Incorporated.

Microsoft, Windows, Windows NT, and the Windows 95 logo are trademarks or registered trademarks of Microsoft Corporation.

UNIX is a registered trademark in the United States and other countries licensed exclusively through X/Open Company Limited.

Other company, product, and service names may be trademarks or service marks of others.

Appendix E. Related Publications

The publications listed in this section are considered particularly suitable for a more general discussion of the topics covered in this redbook.

E.1 International Technical Support Organization Publications

For information on ordering these ITSO publications see "How to Get ITSO Redbooks" on page 165.

- *IBM DSS and DCE Cross-Platform Guide*, SG24-2543
- *Understanding OSF DCE 1.1 for AIX and OS/2*, SG24-4616
- *Security on the Web Using DCE Technology*, SG24-4949
- *Save Surfing: How to Build a Secure WWW Connection*, SG24-4564
- *AIX Version 4.3 Differences Guide*, SG24-2014
- *Load-Balancing Internet Servers*, SG24-4993
- *Building the Infrastructure for the Internet*, SG24-4824
- *The Internet & the World Wide Web: A Time-Saving Guide for New Users*, SG24-2499

E.2 Redbooks on CD-ROMs

Redbooks are also available on CD-ROMs. **Order a subscription** and receive updates 2-4 times a year at significant savings.

CD-ROM Title	Subscription Number	Collection Kit Number
System/390 Redbooks Collection	SBOF-7201	SK2T-2177
Networking and Systems Management Redbooks Collection	SBOF-7370	SK2T-6022
Transaction Processing and Data Management Redbook	SBOF-7240	SK2T-8038
Lotus Redbooks Collection	SBOF-6899	SK2T-8039
Tivoli Redbooks Collection	SBOF-6898	SK2T-8044
AS/400 Redbooks Collection	SBOF-7270	SK2T-2849
RS/6000 Redbooks Collection (HTML, BkMgr)	SBOF-7230	SK2T-8040
RS/6000 Redbooks Collection (PostScript)	SBOF-7205	SK2T-8041
RS/6000 Redbooks Collection (PDF Format)	SBOF-8700	SK2T-8043
Application Development Redbooks Collection	SBOF-7290	SK2T-8037

E.3 Other Publications

These publications are also relevant as further information sources:

- *LDAP: Programming Directory-Enabled Applications with Lightweight Directory Access Protocol*, ISBN 1-57870-000-0

- *X.500 Directory Services; Technology and Deployment*, ISBN 1-85032-879-X

- *LDAP Version 3: The Maturing of the Internet Directory Standard*, The Burton Group, 1998 (may not be available for free)

- *The Advent of Directory-Enabled Computing v2*, The Burton Group, 1995 (may not be available for free)

- *Directory-Enabled Networks Initiative*, The Burton Group, 1997 (may not be available for free)

Please also check Appendix A, "Other LDAP References" on page 139 for more references.

How to Get ITSO Redbooks

This section explains how both customers and IBM employees can find out about ITSO redbooks, CD-ROMs, workshops, and residencies. A form for ordering books and CD-ROMs is also provided.

This information was current at the time of publication, but is continually subject to change. The latest information may be found at http://www.redbooks.ibm.com/.

How IBM Employees Can Get ITSO Redbooks

Employees may request ITSO deliverables (redbooks, BookManager BOOKs, and CD-ROMs) and information about redbooks, workshops, and residencies in the following ways:

- **Redbooks Web Site on the World Wide Web**

  http://w3.itso.ibm.com/

- **PUBORDER** – to order hardcopies in the United States

- **Tools Disks**

  To get LIST3820s of redbooks, type one of the following commands:

  ```
  TOOLCAT REDPRINT
  TOOLS SENDTO EHONE4 TOOLS2 REDPRINT GET SG24xxxx PACKAGE
  TOOLS SENDTO CANVM2 TOOLS REDPRINT GET SG24xxxx PACKAGE (Canadian users only)
  ```

  To get BokkManager BOOKs of redbooks, type the following command:

  ```
  TOOLCAT REDBOOKS
  ```

  To get lists of redbooks, type the following command:

  ```
  TOOLS SENDTO USDIST MKTTOOLS MKTTOOLS GET ITSOCAT TXT
  ```

  To register for information on workshops, residencies, and redbooks, type the following command:

  ```
  TOOLS SENDTO WTSCPOK TOOLS ZDISK GET ITSOREGI 1998
  ```

- **REDBOOKS Category on INEWS**

- **Online** – send orders to: USIB6FPL at IBMMAIL or DKIBMBSH at IBMMAIL

Redpieces

For information so current it is still in the process of being written, look at "Redpieces" on the Redbooks Web Site (http://www.redbooks.ibm.com/redpieces.html). Redpieces are redbooks in progress; not all redbooks become redpieces, and sometimes just a few chapters will be published this way. The intent is to get the information out much quicker than the formal publishing process allows.

How Customers Can Get ITSO Redbooks

Customers may request ITSO deliverables (redbooks, BookManager BOOKs, and CD-ROMs) and information about redbooks, workshops, and residencies in the following ways:

- **Online** Orders – send orders to:

	IBMMAIL	**Internet**
In United States	usib6fpl at ibmmail	usib6fpl@ibmmail.com
In Canada	caibmbkz at ibmmail	lmannix@vnet.ibm.com
Outside North America	dkibmbsh at ibmmail	bookshop@dk.ibm.com

- **Telephone Orders**

United States (toll free)	1-800-879-2755
Canada (toll free)	1-800-IBM-4YOU

Outside North America	(long distance charges apply)
(+45) 4810-1320 - Danish	(+45) 4810-1020 - German
(+45) 4810-1420 - Dutch	(+45) 4810-1620 - Italian
(+45) 4810-1540 - English	(+45) 4810-1270 - Norwegian
(+45) 4810-1670 - Finnish	(+45) 4810-1120 - Spanish
(+45) 4810-1220 - French	(+45) 4810-1170 - Swedish

- **Mail Orders** – send orders to:

IBM Publications	IBM Publications	IBM Direct Services
Publications Customer Support	144-4th Avenue, S.W.	Sortemosevej 21
P.O. Box 29570	Calgary, Alberta T2P 3N5	DK-3450 Allerød
Raleigh, NC 27626-0570	Canada	Denmark
USA		

- **Fax** – send orders to:

United States (toll free)	1-800-445-9269
Canada	1-800-267-4455
Outside North America	(+45) 48 14 2207 (long distance charge)

- **1-800-IBM-4FAX (United States)** or **(+1) 408 256 5422 (Outside USA)** – ask for:

  Index # 4421 Abstracts of new redbooks
  Index # 4422 IBM redbooks
  Index # 4420 Redbooks for last six months

- **On the World Wide Web**

Redbooks Web Site	http://www.redbooks.ibm.com
IBM Direct Publications Catalog	http://www.elink.ibmlink.ibm.com/pbl/pbl

---

Redpieces

For information so current it is still in the process of being written, look at "Redpieces" on the Redbooks Web Site (http://www.redbooks.ibm.com/redpieces.html). Redpieces are redbooks in progress; not all redbooks become redpieces, and sometimes just a few chapters will be published this way. The intent is to get the information out much quicker than the formal publishing process allows.

IBM Redbook Order Form

Please send me the following:

Title	Order Number	Quantity

First name _____ Last name _____

Company _____

Address _____

City _____ Postal code _____ Country _____

Telephone number _____ Telefax number _____ VAT number _____

☐ Invoice to customer number _____

☐ Credit card number _____

Credit card expiration date _____ Card issued to _____ Signature _____

We accept American Express, Diners, Eurocard, Master Card, and Visa. Payment by credit card not available in all countries. Signature mandatory for credit card payment.

List of Abbreviations

ACL	Access Control List	*DTS*	Distributed Time Service
API	Application Programming Interface	*EDI*	Electronic Data Interchange
ASN	Abstract Syntax Notation	*EJB*	Enterprise Java Beans
CA	Certificate Authority	*FTP*	File Transfer Protocol
CCITT	Comite Consultatif International Telephonique et Telegraphique	*GDA*	Global Directory Agent
		GDS	Global Directory Service
CDS	Cell Directory Service (DCE)	*GSO*	Global Sign-On
CRAM-MD5	Challenge-Response Authentication Mechanism - Message Digest 5	*GSSAPI*	Generic Security Service API
		HTTP	Hypertext Transport Protocol
DAP	Directory Access Protocol (X.500)	*IAB*	Internet Architecuture Board
DARPA	Defense Advanced Research Projects Agency	*IANA*	Internet Assigned Numbers Authority
DAS	Directory Assistance Service	*IBM*	International Business Machines Corporation
DCE	Distributed Computing Environment	*IETF*	Internet Engineering Task Force
DEN	Directory Enabled Networks	*IESG*	Internet Engineering Steering Group
DES	Data Encryption Standard	*ISI*	Information Sciences Institute
DIT	Directory Information Tree	*ISO*	International Standards Organization
DN	Distinguished Name	*ISOC*	Internet Society
DNS	Domain Name System	*ITSO*	International Technical Support Organization
DSA	Directory Services Agent	*ITU-T*	International Telecommunications Union - Telecommunications
DSS	Directory & Security Services	*JDAP*	Java Directory Access Protocol (context: Java

	LDAP Application Programming Interface)	**TLS**	Transport Layer Security
JDBC	Java Database Connectivity	**TME**	Tivoli Management Environment
JNDI	Java Naming and Directory Interface (Sun)	**UMICH**	University of Michigan
		URL	Uniform Resource Locator
LAN	Local Area Network	**WAN**	Wide Area Network
LDAP	Lightweight Directory Access Protocol		
LDIF	LDAP Data Interchange Format		
MIME	Multipurpose Internet Mail Extensions		
NDS	Novell Directory Services		
NOS	Network Operating System		
NSI	Name Service Interface (DCE)		
OSF	Open Software Foundation		
OSI	Open Systems Interconnection		
RDN	Relative Distinguished Name		
RFC	Request for Comment		
RPC	Remote Procedure Call		
SASL	Simple Authentication and Security Layer		
SDK	Software Development Kit		
SPI	Service Provider Interface		
SQL	Structured Query Language		
SSL	Secure Sockets Layer		
TCP/IP	Transmission Control Protocol/Internet Protocol		

Index

R

reading 36
referrals 13, 24, 32, 38, 122, 132
relative distinguished name (RDN) 20, 23, 64, 119
Remote Procedure Call, see RPC
replication 6, 69
Request for Comments, see RFC
RFC 11, 12, 131, 142
    1202 12
    1249 12
    1487 12
    1521 45
    1617 64
    1738 122
    1777 12, 15
    1778 12
    1779 12
    1823 13, 85, 145
    1959 12
    1960 12
    2222 45
    2251 13, 15, 22
    2252 13, 22, 28
    2253 13, 22
    2254 13, 23, 94, 96, 127
    2255 13, 23, 85, 120
    2256 13, 23, 28
root DSE 35
RPC 10, 133

S

S/Key 45, 66, 113
SASL 22, 42, 44, 45, 66, 87, 108, 142
scalability 72
schema 21, 27, 60, 61
    subclassing 28
SDK 50, 86, 140, 150
search filter 20, 23, 39, 96, 116
searching 36
security 7, 13, 43, 65, 132
    authentication 7, 41, 66, 68
    authorization 7
    Base64 encoding 44
    basic authentication 44, 108
    Certificate Authority (CA) 48
    SASL 44
    TLS 24, 42
security model 42

server discovery 132, 133
server side sorting 132
Service Provider Interface (SPI) 125
signed directory information 132
single threaded model 113
SMTP 45
Software Development Kit, see SDK
Solaris (Sun) 144, 145
sorting of search results 132
SSL 42, 47, 66, 108, 119, 142, 144, 146
standard schema 61
Structured Query Language (SQL) 4
subclassing 28
suffix 32, 61
Switchboard 151
synchronous mode (API calls) 91

T

TCP/IP 10, 12, 14, 19
telephone directory 2
The Open Group 133
third-party authentication 49
threads 113
threads in DCE 133
Tivoli 141, 147
Tivoli Management Region (TMR) 148
transaction 3
Transport Layer Security (TLS) 24, 42, 113, 142

U

uid attribute 78, 82
unbinding 20
Uniform Resource Locator (URL) 23, 120
University of Michigan 12, 86, 140, 150
update operations 40
URL API 123
userCertificate attribute 81
userPassword attribute 78, 82
UTF-8 22, 52

W

Warp Server domains (IBM) 73
white pages 2, 76
WhoWhere 151
Windows NT (Microsoft) 144, 145
Windows NT/95 domains (Microsoft) 73, 149
World Wide Web 15

ITSO Redbook Evaluation

Understanding LDAP
SG24-4986-00

Your feedback is very important to help us maintain the quality of ITSO redbooks. **Please complete this questionnaire and return it using one of the following methods:**

- Use the online evaluation form found at http://www.redbooks.ibm.com
- Fax this form to: USA International Access Code + 1 914 432 8264
- Send your comments in an Internet note to redbook@us.ibm.com

Which of the following best describes you?
_ **Customer**   _ **Business Partner**   _ **Independent Software Vendor**   _ **IBM employee**
_ **None of the above**

Please rate your overall satisfaction with this book using the scale:
(1 = very good, 2 = good, 3 = average, 4 = poor, 5 = very poor)

Overall Satisfaction   _____

Please answer the following questions:

Was this redbook published in time for your needs?   Yes____ No____

If no, please explain:

_____

_____

_____

_____

What other redbooks would you like to see published?

_____

_____

_____

Comments/Suggestions: **(THANK YOU FOR YOUR FEEDBACK!)**

_____

_____

_____

_____